Leadership
Skills and Stories

Leadership Skills and Stories

A Green Cat Book

Madrid

Publishing History

Green Cat Editorial paperback edition 2018

A Green Cat Book

Publishing History

Green Cat Editorial paperback edition 2018

Published by Green Cat Editorial

Madrid, Madrid

Copyright © 2018 Brendan Anglin

The moral right of the author has been asserted

Copyright © 2018 Brendan Anglin

ISBN 978-84-944194-3-0

Dedicated to my father.

When everything is going well a true leader stands behind their followers. When everything is going badly, they stand in front.

Contents

Introduction:

The leaders around us

It is amazing what you can accomplish if you do not care who gets the credit

Harry Truman

Barack Obama, Gandhi, Joan of Arc. Fortune 500 company CEOs. Presidents of countries. Military leaders. Visionary entrepreneurs. There is plenty written about each of these, and, there is no doubt that they are all excellent examples of leaders. The problem, however, with these figures that appear in newspapers, business journals and history books is that most people see them on a pedestal but cannot see the steps that lead up to them. When ordinary people study them they see them as ideals rather than real examples of how they can be leaders - here, now and in their own lives.

This book sets out to change that – giving clear skills that a leader should and can develop, practical steps to take, and then stories of real leaders in a variety of contexts as seen through the eyes of young people who are on the road to becoming leaders themselves.

The style of writing that runs through this book is something that I would call 'confident vulnerability'. This style means that neither I nor the other authors of this book do not claim to be perfect, leading experts on the subject or have the answers to everything. However, we are confident that in the area of Leadership no-one has all the answers and that the best way to find your path to leadership is to experience and witness as many examples as possible, with all their vulnerabilities exposed. Sometimes an honest, imperfect story gives you a better roadmap than a perfect lie. We have also written in a natural style that should read more like a conversation on paper than an inaccessible academic volume.

Leadership is not something that everyone agrees on – like gravity or how good Spanish food is! Rather it is a concept that has a thousand definitions, interpretations and theories. To a young women or man the result of having so many theoretical interpretations is that they study Leadership as a subject that will appear on an exam rather than a living, pulsing part of their lives and the lives of everyone they know[1].

---

[1] When you put down this book and decide which one to read next I suggest, rather than reading a book about Leadership per se, that you start with the bestselling classic "The 7 Habits of Highly Effective people" by Steven Covey. While we cover leadership skills (including personality traits) in the book you are reading now, it is also important to develop the necessary character to be a leader for all of your life and not just particular situations. "The 7 Habits' is an excellent primer in this area and has changed the lives of many people for the better. While it is not specifically a

This book takes the approach that Leadership is something that can be learned and developed and that depending on the situation and context one leadership style works better than another. It is divided into sections based around specific skills all leaders possess, from personalities to vision to trust. It combines the theories and thoughts of many thinkers on Leadership (you can find a recommended reading list at the back of the book[2]) with "Key Takeaways" and an example of a real world leader.

All of the leaders covered in these stories have been contacted and interviewed directly by the authors and written in a way that shows the authors' experience of what a leader is. The individual viewpoints they provide, and the vantage point of young people who want to be leaders into the 21st Century themselves, gives an original and refreshing glimpse of what leaders are actually like.

The Changing face of leadership

In the 21st Century when information is readily available, change happens faster than many people's ability to adapt, and traditional ideologies are no longer the uniting forces for

---

'leadership' book, it does talk about becoming the type of person that we need more of in leadership positions.

[2] For an excellent general overview of Leadership theories with case studies on each of the main leadership "schools" go with Peter G. Northouse's book "Leadership." It does not cover the 'how to' of leadership but rather the theoretical framework and background that surrounds the study of leadership.

groups that they once were, there is a greater need for leadership than ever before[3].

In the past, when roles, hierarchies and organisations were clearly established, the world needed many managers: People who were effective, efficient and process driven. Money was considered by many as the prime motivator, despite the existence of a plethora of theories on motivation that said the opposite. Human resources treated people precisely as that – resources.

Leaders were considered something that you found at the top of the organisation, not at every level of the organisation. It was believed that what was needed was management skills, not leadership skills. Young people entered the workforce, focused on moving up the corporate ladder, motivated by salary increases, bonuses and promotions. You had to learn at the bottom, make your mistakes, put in your time and energy, work hard and climb or sometimes claw your way to the top.

Charismatic leaders like Jack Welch, Lee Iacoca and even Steve Jobs were the exemplary leaders held up for people to be inspired by. Leadership was something that leaders did and everyone knew that leaders were at the top of the ladder or the pyramid. Despite the copious literature that argues against

---

[3] "Thank you for being late" by Thomas Friedman discusses this era of rapid change we are living in and the need to learn HOW to adapt and develop a growth mind-set rather than just learning information that is soon outdated.

this very limited vision of what leadership is, most often when I ask people what a leader is today, they give the same examples and same ideas as 10, 20, 30 and 50 years ago.

What is slightly surprizing is that in 2018, the vast majority of the leaders that they mention to me are male, 40+ and overwhelmingly Caucasian. When they are not Caucasian, they are generally from the United States. All of the people they talk about are indeed leaders, and wonderful examples, but the range of choices are surprisingly limited. When I ask for a non-Caucasian example of a business leader they give me Tony Hsieh of Zappo shoes[4]. What I am hoping they will say is someone like Jack Ma[5]. When I ask for a non-male example they give me Sheryl Sandberg but not Ellen Johnson Sirleaf[6].

---

[4] Tony Hsieh sold his first Company LinkExchange to Microsoft at the age of 24 for $265 million. He then went on to transform and become the CEO of Zappos. His book 'Delivering Happiness' is a wonderful read, regardless of whether you sign up to everything he says, on the areas of positive leadership and creating a happy workforce that delivers great results.

[5] Jack Ma is of course the incredible entrepreneur and philanthropist and founder and driving force behind Alibaba, a combination of Bill Gates, Jeff Bezos and Elon Musk. For more about this man who started out as a humble English teacher I recommend Duncan Clark's book "Alibaba: the House that Jack built."

[6] I would strongly recommend Sandberg's, COO of Facebook's, inspiring book "Lean In" which talks about women and leadership. For more on Ellen Johnson Sirleaf, Nobel Peace Prize winner and former president of Liberia I would read Helene Cooper's book 'Madame President'.

They certainly do not look around at the people they know personally and see on a daily basis and point and say 'That person is a leader.'

When you decide that leadership is something that people do every day, in all walks of life, at all ages, you realise that you are surrounded by living examples. When you see the leadership qualities of the people that form a part of your life you can learn from them and become a better leader yourself.

Each of these people may excel in a different area of leadership but by observing what they do well and learning in a structured way you can develop all of their skills and transform your own leadership abilities.

Level 5 and Servant Leaders

Jim Collins, in his book "Good to Great", talks about the enduring success of certain companies. The study looked at the outliers, the companies that consistently performed ahead of the market over a period of many years. To his own surprize the element that all of these companies had in common was a particular type of Leader.

He called this particular type of Leader, a level 5 leader. These Level 5 Leaders were not charismatic leaders who led through the force of their personality, taking centre stage, personally very ambitious and regularly in these headlines. They were personally humble but extremely ambitious for the organisations that they led. They were highly focused and ensured that everyone that followed them was equally focused. Rather than moulding people into the right jobs, they identified the right people and then developed the jobs.

Many of the headline grabbing charismatic leaders did not create a succession policy, sometimes deliberately, so then when they left and someone else took over, their companies suffered or even nosedived. They look good, but their organisations suffer.

Instead of that selfish approach, a Level 5 leader creates a leadership organization that continues to grow even when they have left. As Jim Collins says a Level 5 Leader is "an individual who blends extreme personal humility with intense professional will."[7]

Servant Leadership was a term that was originally coined by Robert K. Greenleaf in 1970. According to an article he wrote at that time the main difference between a servant as leader and leader first is

> "the care taken by the servant - first to make sure that other people's highest priority needs are being served.

---

[7] Good To Great and Level 5 Leadership fits in the group of Leadership theories called 'Trait Leadership'. Traditionally this was the type of leadership that focused on great leaders and then tried to find what personality traits or characteristics they had in common. In recent decades there has been a return to favour of this type of leadership theory with the idea that that people can develop these traits (as opposed to behaviours). We look in more detail at personalities in a later chapter.

The best test, and difficult to administer, is: Do those served grow as persons? Do they, while being served, become healthier, wiser, freer, more autonomous, more likely themselves to become servants? And, what is the effect on the least privileged in society? Will they benefit or at least not be further deprived?"[8]

Larry Spears in 2002[9] identified ten characteristics of Servant Leadership in Greenleaf's work and each of these areas are reflected in distinct sections of this book as skills and areas that can be developed. Listening, Empathy, Healing (concern for the well-being of followers), Awareness (of context and environment – physical and social), Persuasion, Conceptualization (vision), Foresight, Stewardship (taking responsibility for their followers, the organisation and the 'greater good of society'), Commitment to the growth of people, and Building community. [10] This is the type of leadership that we believe the 21st Century needs more of.

---

[8] Greenleaf, R.K. (1970). The Servant as Leader. This extract is taken from the Centre for Servant Leadership website: https://www.greenleaf.org/what-is-servant-leadership/
[9] This summary of the main characteristics of this leadership style and Spear's article "Tracing the past, present, and future of servant-leadership." *Focus on Leadership: Servant-leadership for the 21st Century* (2002) is taken from Northouse's (2016) analysis of Servant Leadership.
[10] A more accessible book in this area is 'Leaders Eat last' by Simon Sinek (2014)

You will also find that all of the leaders that appear in this book display many or all of the traits of a Level % Servant Leader.

*

The aim of this book is that by looking at the leadership characteristics of normal but extraordinary people you can begin to get a sense of how it is possible to develop a lens and filter through which you can appreciate the leadership qualities of others – and therefore learn from them and grow with them.

So let us start this discovery of what it means and what it takes to be a leader.   And where better place to start than with Vision.

1

Vision

Leadership is the capacity to translate vision into reality.

Warren Bennis

The message is clear the moment you read the title of the book. Simon Sinek tells all leaders who are trying to motivate both external and internal followers what they must do – "Start with Why". He successfully shows how organisations and individuals who inspire and motivate others to travel the journey with them do not describe their mission in terms of 'what' they do, or even 'how' they do it, but rather 'why' they do it.[11] The Golden Circle he talks about goes from 'Why' at the centre, to 'how' and then 'what'.

When we are talking about leadership this *Why* describes the vision that unites everyone behind them. As one of the leading experts on Leadership, Walter Bennis, points out, it is this

---

[11] Before you decide to read his book you can watch his Ted Talk at https://www.youtube.com/watch?v=u4ZoJKF_VuA

understanding of 'why' that differentiates a leader from a manager who focuses more on 'what' and 'how'.

Steven Covey illustrates this even better when he talks about people cutting down trees in a forest. The manager gets everyone to cut faster and more efficiently. The leader, however, climbs to the top of the tallest tree, looks out and then cries to the rest 'wrong forest.' Managers get us up the ladder faster, leaders make sure that the ladder is against the right wall.[12]

What does a vision entail?

When constructing a vision for your organisation and people it is have to have several elements:

- Relevance
- Motivating and Inspiring
- Clear and Specific

By relevant we mean that the vision directly connects with the desires of the followers. They believe that it is something that will change their lives and the lives of others. If they feel that the primary objective of your vision is selfish and is only about your needs then this vision will not work. The only way you can get them to follow your vision if this is the case is through carrots and sticks. Carrots in the form of high pay will buy their

---

[12] Steven Covey covers this area in the section 'start with the end in mind' of his book 'the 7 Habits of Highly Effective People.'

bodies but not their hearts. Sticks in the form of threats or the use of direct authority will own their bodies but not their hearts. In the 21st century people work for companies that are aligned with their perception of themselves and their values. This means that when creating a vision for your organisation, you must create it with your followers (they can be part of the process but not generally the final decision makers) or you find and hire people who believe in that vision.

The vision should be motivating to the extent that it links to their intrinsic desires (see the chapter on motivation later in this book). This way it will also bring a team together and keep them working to fulfil the vision even when the going gets tough. To discover whether it is motivating or not you should ask yourself if you would be motivated by it in their shoes (not yours). Is there an emotional element to the vision – does it speak to their hearts as well as their minds? When they go to work on this vision do they feel they are truly part of something bigger, and that the something bigger is making a difference in the world? If not, if they are simply turning up to be physically present, to get a pay check, then it is time to rethink your vision.

It should also be clear, concrete and specific[13]. 'We want to be the best in our industry' means nothing. 'Best' at what? Profits,

---

[13] In "Made to Stick" by Chip and Dan Heath, where 'sticky' ideas are covered in detail, one of the key ideas is to make the idea 'concrete'. That means that people can actually vizualise in their mind's eye what you are talking about. Steve Jobs, when he talked about the IPod, could have described it as an MP3 player with

market share, safety, quality, customer satisfaction? 'in our industry' – what does that mean? What is your sector?

Writing a vision (not mission) statement means locking into words the dreams that are swirling around in your head. The problem of course is that many people then take their initial vision and put it in corporate speak which is full of buzzwords but does not speak to people, and certainly not your followers. Legally and technically the vision statement might be correct but the life and soul of it has been drained away.

It helps to take a maximum of three key words that describe your objectives and ensure that whenever anyone hears your vision statement, or some form of it, they are left with those three key words ringing in their head. Even better if you can get it down to one word like 'safety.'

When Paul O'Neill became the CEO of Alcoa in 1987 he announced that 'I intend to make Alcoa the safest company in America. I intend to go for zero injuries.'[14] There were no buzzwords, no abstract, unworkable concepts that people could not understand. And then he proceeded to drive that message home again and again at all levels. That one key message was very relevant to the workers at Alcoa where work related accidents often led to death and mutilation. In the

---

maximum storage but instead he used the expression 'a 1,000 songs in your pocket.' How can you make the vision so obvious that people can imagine it in front of them?

[14] The Power of Habit, Charles Duhigg. Pg. 98

same vein it is also extremely motivating – it was literally a message that would spell the difference between life and death for many employees.

Commander's Intent

This is a term that is used in the military to describe the overall objective of the top commander in the battlefield. "What is it that we are supposed to achieve as a collective in this campaign?" When everyone knows the overarching 'why' of the commander individual units, from battalions down to a single private understands what they have to do and can therefore modify their own behaviour accordingly and adapt to the many unexpected situations that occur in the midst of battle.

Many low-cost airline companies have a commander's intent of not doing anything that will cost the company, and therefore their customers, any money. Everyone who works for the airline knows this. This means that when a customer asks a flight attendant for something the individual employee is able to do a quick mental check "will this cost the company?" If it does, then they do not give it to the customer, if it does not, they will. By understanding this overall 'why' of the company, it is not necessary to prepare for every possible eventuality, which would be impossible. When followers have a clear idea of what the vision is and are on board with it, then they can put the vision into practice even when the leader is not there to remind them.

Finding time to think

This is one of the most difficult things that a leader can do. Getting away from being busy and creating the mental space to come away from the present and imagine. One strategy that leaders are increasingly doing is taking 'digital holidays' where they go somewhere for a week without access to the internet. This allows them to reduce external distractions and actually think about the big picture.

An alternative, daily practice is mindfulness and meditation. This allows us to step back and look at the forest and not just caught up in the details of the trees. In a word where we find ourselves deep in the forest most of the day, with constant new vegetation growing up around us, it can be exceedingly difficult to keep the vision in mind.

However, if you are finding it difficult, then you can imagine the people who are following you. They need their leaders to keep one eye on the road and make sure that the car is being driven by someone who know where everyone else is going.

Later in the chapter on setting goals we will look at how to bring a vision from statement to strategy.

Key Takeways

1. People need a vision to inspire them
2. It is a leader's responsibility to ensure that there is a vision and not being busy.
3. The vision should be relevant, motivating and specific.
4. Try and keep the main ideas to three, or even better – One.
5. By handing an overall direction that everyone is heading in, people know how to react in unexpected circumstances as their reactions will either take them closer or farther away from their goal.
6. It is necessary to find time to think and get distance in order to be sure of the vision your followers need.

2

Fjord

Leading through vision

Saad Benkirane

Lucas Mateu

Introduction

Disrupting a long-established sector is never easy, and the consulting one is no exception. With very closed rules and standardised methods, this 130 year old professional practice is quite restricted in terms of creativity and ways of working; it is very much like a handbook that limited high level firms follow. We've been amazed at how Fjord, a company that was initially relatively small in size and capital, was able to lead a whole industry into a new way of thinking, and embracing innovation and design; ultimately helping make products and services that users love . From what we've seen and heard from Fjord directly, there are definitely a lot of approaches that can be real game changers when it comes to bridging the gap with the digital world, and all in all becoming a better company. We wanted to share our thoughts on those that impacted us most, and that we identified as key aspects to their vision of leading the industry to a great new place where beliefs become a reality.

For Fjord, being a leader isn't purely about running a successful business. It's about understanding what's happening in the environment they operate in, and seizing opportunities as soon as they present themselves. We have to be able to take advantage of the technology that surrounds us, and that means that we can no longer think in the same way. We have to bring products and services to life by redesigning people's relationships with the world around them. It is no longer about what "you" want, but what "we" want: co-creating a vision for yourself and for others. In fact, even when asked if they considered themselves leaders, some of their staff's instinct was to talk about how they helped their clients innovate, rather than about themselves, pursuing innovation directly as a company objective. Although ultimately, one leads to the other, and they naturally become leaders in what they do.

Having said this, and before jumping into their key factors, it is important to understand what it is that they do. At the end of the day Fjord helps companies think and create new products and services through a process called "service design": a holistic activity that analyses how a system works on every level (actors, interactions, infrastructure, etc.) to create a better experience and a better run business. Fjord has clearly identified its core values and ensures that everything that they do revolves around and leads from those values. In a nutshell, their six guiding lights are elegant simplicity (intuitive and appealing design), fun and collaboration (a working dynamic that champions collaboration and co-creation), emotion and logic (align with the user, be empathetic), curiosity (experiment whenever and wherever: cross disciplinary, cross cultural and cross industry), constant innovation (produce one of kind solutions geared to be the best), and last but not least, design evolution (there is always room for improvement).

Becoming a living business: the company culture.

Culture is definitely one of Fjord's most important areas we analysed. The world we now live in changes every millisecond, and that means that one's ability to respond to this constant change will be the determinant of one's leadership in its field. Fjord recognised the need to respond quickly to a changing environment and noted the paramount importance of remaining fresh and relevant in their industry. This meant they needed new knowledge and new expertise, and fortunately, their strategy shifted to allow the whole company to keep moving forward. "Fjord is constantly changing: every new person that joins our team and every client we work with brings something new. We evolve with the world around us."

Obviously this sounds great on paper, but without some core values, it would have been impossible for Fjord to scale and maintain the proper functioning of the company throughout the years. Our research and insight into this, repeatedly brought up 2 tendencies amongst employees: being bold and being generous. These really seem to be the principles that not only empower them to work with a diverse global team, but to work "together as one".

Generosity at Fjord comes in three shapes: collaboration, transparency and empathy. By working hand in hand in a supportive community, everyone contributes on behalf of the team, and celebrates breakthroughs collectively. This really helps communicate the vision and show (not only say) what it is all about. Fitting in with their "unfailingly honest", direct and open way to do business, their efforts in trying to be as transparent as possible both with Fjordians and with customers, puts forward what they do and the reason behind it. Last, but evidently not least, comes their curiosity to learn from others. Their best work relies on diverse perspectives and experiences, and this pushes them to relentlessly open their ears and minds, and put themselves in other's shoes: empathy at its greatest.

Being visionaries, adventurous and impactful, Fjordians are clearly bold leaders. Their passion for what they do -creating stirring new solutions- and their propensity to face uncertainty and complexity with a sense of fun and exploration, puts them at the forefront of their industry. They commit to creating "meaningful change that leaves things better" than how they found them, and that is a strong commitment, to say the least.

Operating internationally means facing international issues: and despite what one may think, language isn't the most critical aspect, culture is. When you're doing business in another culture, understanding individual personality is not enough to avoid potential conflict; you also have to understand the foundations of the culture where you're doing business, and this means understanding how they communicate, how they trust, how they decide and even how they lead. The context where the communication is happening, the emotions that accompany it, and more important than ever, the personal touch one has, creates a situation in which one has to play with different parameters to ensure success. And in the age of personalisation, expectations are much higher when it comes to personal treatment and awareness of the other. Fjord's presence in multiple regions around the world allows them to prepare "aware leaders" that can be flown around the world with confidence, knowing they will be able to operate no matter the culture; ultimately allowing them to develop Cross-cultural Leadership throughout the organisation, on which we will discuss further later. For us, international students at a university where there are more than 80 nationalities, we now understand how important this is in the world of business.

FJORD Evolution

Also notable was a division at Fjord, created in response to their awareness of globalisation and cultural diversity. "Our response is Fjord Evolution, a global team dedicated to enabling our diverse people to harness and expand their skills, and bring their personalities and passion together, as One."

So as to teach Fjordians and clients about service design thinking, powerful methods, creative leadership and craft skills, FJORD Evolution organises inspiring talks and workshops, and puts together a digital repository of tools and wisdom. We would love to be able to have these type of tools in our future work environments, creating unique learning experiences where we cultivate a unique ethos.

Styles of Leadership within Fjord

What Fjord has understood is that being a leader is more than merely running a successful business, but it is about the attributes and the established set of attitudes that come with it. It is about understanding that a lack of communication, accountability, alignment, clear vision, poor company culture, amongst other factors will guide their vision towards a defected path.

Fjord's company culture is an important factor that helped them be the leaders they are today. The values that encompass their culture inspires a blend of transformational leadership, with foundational roots of cross-cultural leadership.

(1. Transformational Leadership)

Fjord strongly believes in initiating change within the company. Being leaders in innovation, they have to advance in parallel, if not further, to their environment. Every new addition to the team – from new Fjordians, to new clients – bring novel ideas and different perspectives to the table. This encourages an open mind to new train of thoughts and point of views. Also, Fjord constantly sets demanding expectations to motivate their teams to surpass their capabilities in every front of a project, resulting in top-level performance. This strategy contributes to the personal growth of team members, by making them capable of taking on greater responsibilities. As a source of empowerment, it becomes apparent that they are valued by their community and that they are efficient resources. Nonetheless, in the middle of continuous change, their values remain identical.

(2. Cross-cultural Leadership)

Having a leadership team from around the globe brings on diverse cultures that are not necessarily interchangeable. Fjord has leaders that can effectively adapt their methods of leadership based on the different cultures from Europe, North & Latin America, Australia, and Asia. They all work together to spread and expose Fjordians to the distinct cultures. With the different ways of thinking and perspectives this entails, Fjord has opened themselves to learn from other cultures and rely on the diversity to add value and inspire their clients.

Leading with others

Working with others unlocks a path where simple ideas can transform themselves into tangible, co-created products and services. We envisioned this as the essence of their ability to create vision for others. The cross-pollination of thoughts that reshapes what was once a mental picture into an outcome that would not have been attainable if attempted alone.

The basis of working in unison revolves around communication: the sharing of knowledge and ideas for the future, and most importantly, the creation of strong relationships. These relationships will be the component that will change these 'conversations' into action. This is the fundamental perspective of Fjord that helps shape their vision.

Obviously it was important for us to note that Fjord had been acquired by Accenture Interactive, gaining a greater worldwide reachability, and substantially increased the size of their design team. Because however positive an impact this had on the company, this was solely a lipstick operation (and that is how they saw it, not our opinion). They might have grown in size, but they still felt the need for something greater that would help them flourish. Something that will push the company to the next level, and allow them to reach their full potential. That being the case, Fjord saw the opportunity to exploit this relationship with Accenture to a deeper extent, where they would fully quench their thirst of innovation by seeking greater opportunities. An ecosystem of leading with others was henceforth established. They began with a partnership with

Matter, an innovative product design company. This allowed Fjord to now have the ability to create physical products for their clients through the service design and strategies they provide. Now, not only are they able to help businesses achieve what they seek, but they can provide them with the suggested product itself. Although this was a big step, this was not the end for Fjord, whose ambition craved to expand its network. What came next in Fjord's vision was to enlarge the creativity of their environment. Thus, the merger with Chaotic Moon: a creative technology studio that focuses on developing technologies such as drones and technological tattoos. While it wasn't clear what the value added of the company would be to Fjord, this bet for innovation enabled them to expand their stream of knowledge in rapid prototyping and creative technology capabilities; something that today is an essential part of their core competencies for their project developments.

We believe that what Fjord has done could have been for the worst. Having three different company cultures working within one entity could have arisen impactful communication issues, where the mission and vision of the company wouldn't have been shared within all three businesses. Yet, Fjord was successful in persuading the newly added teams to accept and embrace Fjord's vision and mission, by making it their own. They were able to completely change the denotation of "my vision" to "our vision", from an "I", to a "we". With Matter, Fjord built such a trust by reinforcing it through non-verbal actions. With the merger of Chaotic Moon, Matter was able to comfortably reach a higher level of innovation by making full use of the new added expertise. This co-benefited Fjord and Matter. They were both able to grow with the help of each other, leading the way to innovation.

The Fjordian Model of Innovation.

Leading by mistake?

Fjord's underlying principle of their service is having a customer-experience-led approach rather than a platform-led approach. What Fjord seeks to accomplish is to create a relationship between the customers and the service or product they use. Fjord thrives to become the value differential, through understanding what the customers want. Rather than following the current trends in the technology world, and implementing them within any solution they provide to their clients, Fjord determines the technologies that will have an apparent impact in the way the customers interact with the different industries, and they keep them in their toolkit in case it would make sense to use them. Nowadays, buzzwords can be used by anyone, and trends can be implemented everywhere. Blockchain, artificial intelligence, augmented reality, the list goes on and on. What differs these players from Fjord, is that Fjordians progress more in depth, and take the step further, asking themselves if the technology streamlines the customer journey. Will it become an experience the user loves?

This reveals the core values Fjord has recognized. They not only listen to the wishes of their clients, but they ensure that special attention is given to the customers of those clients. In order to do so, Fjord has gone deeper than just the surface of their clients. They went to a customer level where they would clearly understand what the customers go through every day to use the product. Through that, Fjord established an environment where their values are what drives their actions. From understanding the customer journey, to having conversations with them to gain greater insight makes the service Fjord provides perspicuously customer-focused.

Fjord hence grasps greater insight on how to lead their clients towards the right path of leadership and success, through adjusting some processes based on what is wanted, and needed for the users. Together with the users, Fjord has shed to light a leading relationship where the shared goal is the growth and success of the business in hand.

Reengineering the company from the inside out

What is fascinating with Fjord is that the value they have established in terms of cultural transformation has been prompted by changing their own company culture. Throughout our studies in the business world, we came to understand that driving innovation from the outside, by looking in, is no longer effective. Recommending changes that will only alter the outer layer of the company is not something that will help them develop the attributes of effective leadership. This stands behind the idea that we are not born a leader, but we become one. To become leaders of meaningful innovation, what companies, and especially what Fjord embraced, is re-engineering the company from the inside out.

One problem we believe will be encountered is internal opposition. Change is something that people constantly reject, from our personal lives to our professional ones. Something that goes against what you are familiar and comfortable with will not be received favourably. With that in mind, all businesses seek to drive innovation; and by definition, innovation is all about change. It is about taking a different approach to develop something that was once familiar.

In most cases, businesses turn to partners for recommendations to introduce a novel way of thinking. This is the easy option, whatever new ways of thinking the partners will recommend might be seen as innovative for the host company, as it might be something the outsourcer is familiar with within their own company.

However, this will limit the spectrum of possible change just because the initiatives led by third parties is not a change the employees thought of themselves. It is something they believe is unnecessary and will lead to resistance. This is completely normal nevertheless. Think of it this way: when the human body recognizes a 'foreign body', it sends signals and acts to expel the foreign body in order to re-establish equilibrium.

"Businesses should turn to partners not just to recommend change, but to install them within the organisation to spread new methods, tools and strategies via cultural change."

Mark Curtis, Chief Client Officer at FJORD

Being a company that experienced this circumstance, Fjord empathizes with the fear companies have towards the risk of having internal opposition. They haven't come up with a secret path to innovation through analysing different companies and gather all this information into one. But they recognized it though their own experiences. They are leading others through their own past struggles. Fjord has converted this fear, uncertainty, and doubt they once had to establish their core values that define them as leaders today.

Transparency:

Keeping the promise.

For many years, "the definition of a brand essentially amounted to a promise, but what is a promise worth if it is not kept, which is to say, if we fail to deliver it through customer experience and services?" There was really no better way of putting it here, than to quote Fjord themselves. With the arrival of digital, customers have found it increasingly difficult to trust brands: what will they do with our personal data? Will they sell it to Facebook? Will someone have access to my credit card number? Will I get hacked? To be honest, users have the right to be concerned for their safety, and they should be. From what we've been seeing over the last years, is no longer a question of "if" someone is going to attack and land on our data, but "when" will it happen, and that is why brands should be as transparent as possible: communicating in a fast and precise way, not like what we've seen in the past with countless amount of data leaks situations (Sony, Yahoo, Uber, LinkedIn). The issue here is that sometimes it's not a question of willingness, but more about the ability to execute this objective of transparency. Do companies have the right audit systems in place? If they do, are they designed correctly? Do they actively invest in cybersecurity?

So obviously with more demanding customers in terms of transparency and standards, more than ever, "brand promises must translate into tangible experiences". The Facebook and Cambridge Analytica scandal are a perfect example of what should never happen, and Fjord are helping their clients keep prevent these situations by designing better, in every aspect, and being ready to act in the right way in the unfortunate scenario that something does happen. Nowadays, "a brand is what it does". What it delivers now counts more than what it promises, and "experience has become the essential yardstick. It is the route to keeping brand promises and enabling brands to emerge in a highly digitalised world".

Conclusion

We believe all of these factors are what position FJORD as a leader in their sector, and if they keep moving forward with this mentality and build an army of thinkers, they will go very, very far. And for us personally, this is honestly the perfect environment in which we could wish to work in.

References:

Fjord website, blog –

https://www.fjordnet.com/conversations/the-need-to-connect-brand-experience-with-customer-experience/

Fjord website, cases –

https://www.fjordnet.com/workdetail/unilever-reimagining-the-employee-experience/

Fjord on Twitter - https://twitter.com/fjord

Fjord website, About Us –

https://www.fjordnet.com/about-us/we-believe/

The culture map, 42 Fresh Ideas –

https://www.youtube.com/watch?v=uENuOPWP1CM

3

Understanding Others

When the best leader's work is done the people say, 'We did it ourselves.'

Lao Tzu

There is no one truth, and life is about finding yours. Some of us are under the illusion that reality is what we perceive. If you hold this belief, and the accompanying belief that therefore everyone else perceives reality the same way as you do, or else they are wrong, will create a myriad of problems for you as a leader.

From a philosophical background we can use Plato's analogy that we are simply shadows cast on the cave wall by others. Stretching this idea into the realm of leadership means that we must understand that we only see part of the picture. Occasionally the part of the picture that we see coincides with what others also see. In fact, we have a tendency to surround ourselves with people who see the world we do. And very often we also subtly adapt our own perception to reflect the views of the groups we find ourselves in (or choose to follow[15]).

This filter, through which we perceive reality, is influenced by our age, our gender, our nationality, our economic status, our knowledge in that moment, our mood, and where our attention is, among other things. A leader takes all of these filters into account when dealing with their followers.

In the previous chapter we looked at Vision. When a leader creates a Vision, they can do it in line with what the followers already believe, or they can open their eyes to a new possibility. In the second case they have to understand what their followers' current filters are in order to know how to communicate that vision and to understand how they are changing as a result of this vision.

---

[15] Kevin Dutton cites one striking experiment where people formed part of a group of people who were identifying whether a colour was green or blue. Unknown to the people in the experiment, everyone else in the group was part of the experimenter's team. When something was clearly green, the rest of the group would call out that it was blue. It was found that the one individual who was not part of the group started to shout out the same colour as the rest. So far this can be put down to peer pressure. However, testing later, separately, showed that the person had actually changed their perception of the colour. You can find this experiment and many others that show how easy it is to manipulate people in Dutton's book 'Flipnosis'.

Benefits of understanding others

- Communicating vision in a way that registers with them.
- Motivate them the way they need to be motivated, not the way you would be.
- Anticipate synergies and problems of putting them in a team together.
- See what they might perceive as obstacles in the achievement of your vision, and then help to clear those obstacles from the path.
- Build trust.
- Manage emotions in difficult circumstances.
- Have an insight into what makes them tick when persuasion and negotiation must be used.

In 1979 Patricia Moore, a young designer who was only 26 at the time, went so far as to dress herself up as an 85 year old woman (complete with glasses that made it difficult to see and a costume that restricted her movement) in order to see the world through the eyes of an old person moving through the city[16]. It is not necessary for a leader to go to that extent to

---

[16] This example comes from Roman Krznaric's book 'Empathy', a manifesto which clearly shows the benefits (including health) to the individual and to society as a whole of an increase in empathy – and practical steps for how to achieve this. In a digitally connected world we are paradoxically more aware of what everyone else is thinking and also less emotionally affected by that knowledge.

understand how their followers perceive the world, but an increase in empathy and perspective taking can only improve their leadership skills. This can take the form of working for a day at the same job to simply sitting down and chatting with the followers and listening to them.

Personalities

One of the ways of simplifying the task of understanding potentially thousands of people is to break them down into groups. One of the ways of doing this is by using broad stroke ideas of personalities. Before I go deeper into this section I would like to point out that when it comes to personalities I err on the side of caution. Personalities are not necessarily fixed permanently, nor are personality tests 100% accurate descriptors of who we are and how we will act in specific situations. Having said that, they do give an idea of how different people perceive the world and to take those differences into account.

There are many ways of classifying personalities so the objective of this section is not to cover them all but to give a taste of how they might change your interaction with your followers.

Carl Jung divided personalities using three opposing scales[17]. The first was introvert and extravert. These basically talk about whether individuals are energized by spending time with others or not. If you have a team of introverts then they will need time to work on their own, quiet time, and thinking time. Otherwise they will become exhausted and not work to their full potential. It is important to recognise that being an introvert does not necessarily mean you are not good at dealing with other people, simply that you find your energy draining away the more time you are surrounded by interactive others.

An extravert, on the other hand, is energized by spending time with others. Team work and group activities fill them with life. Face-to-face meetings, social interaction and regular interaction will keep them engaged. It is also worth remembering that just because someone likes to be with other people that this does not automatically mean that they are Emotionally Intelligent, diplomatic individuals. They might be terrible at handling interpersonal situations and revel in conflict, but love the energy they get from these situations.

---

[17] You can of course read Carl Jung in the original German but I found that James Borg, in his book *Persuasion*, covers Carl Jung's Personality types in a very clear, comprehensive and applicable way. You will also find that Carl Jung's personality types have strongly influenced the creation of commonly used personality models such as the Myers-Briggs Personality Type Indicator and the 16 Personalities typology.

If you have a team that is made up of both types of individuals then you will have to take this into account and act as a balancing influence between them and when it comes to task assignment and construction.

The second scale Carl Jung used was about how people gather information – are they Sensers or Intuiters. A Senser will rely on what they can see and touch, on personal direct experience. You will have to give them concrete examples and visible applications of what you are saying. An Intuiter however works with their imagination, abstract ideas, possibilities of what could be rather than what they can physically grab a hold of.

The third scale is how people then take decisions. Carl Jung divides people here into Thinkers and Feelers – whether people use hard facts, logic and data to take their decisions (Thinkers) or if they take into account emotions, intuition, and other people when taking decisions.

As you can imagine – leading a sense based, emotional, extravert is completely different in every way (from communication, to motivation) to leading an abstract thinking, logical introvert. There will be a natural tendency to prefer to deal with the people who reflect your personality traits but a true leader knows how to adapt to every personality.

Other studies show that there are differences between the way individuals handle conflict, stress and anxiety, competitive/cooperative behaviour, risk and uncertainty, degrees of conscientiousness, detail versus general picture etc.

The first step however in understanding others (apart from the step of understanding oneself) is empathy and a willingness to accept the fact that we do not all perceive the world through the same lens.

The LMX (Leader-Member Exchange Theory) by Graen et al takes this focus on the relationship between the leader and the individual and converts it into a working theory. Rather than treating the leader as 'leading a group' it focuses on the dyadic links between the leader and the individual follower, and the natural tendency for some individuals to fall into the 'in-group' and others into the "out group" based in part on similarities between the leader and the follower. This theory gives practical ideas about how to move people from the 'out-group' to the 'in-group' and one element of that is recognising the individual relationship that exists in each case.[18]

Key Takeaways

1. Focus on the other first.
2. Understand where they are coming from.
3. Identify their communication style.
4. Take into account how they use emotions, or react in emotional situations.
5. Understand what motivates them.

---

[18] For a detailed overview of the LMX theory you can go to https://www.researchgate.net/publication/290821113_LMX_differentiation_Understanding_relational_leadership_at_individual_and_group_levels

6. Identify the differences as a potential source of conflict and maximise similarities as a point of rapport.

7. As a leader you must leave your own self at the door unless it helps to create a sense of empathy and bonds.

8. A leader cares about followers but does not expect the followers to care about the leader.

9. Once all of this is identified it is possible to strip them away to discover what the other person is really saying.

10. Conversely when communicating back with an individual all of those layers can be added on and woven through the message to make it more effective.

4

Vladimir Liakhovitch

Bastien Le Bretton

John Lebo

Louis Lechanteur

Victoria Irazu Oliva

Anastasia Novikova

Being a leader is not about being on top or being the most popular, it is about learning to work with other people and putting the groups' needs above your own and guiding people towards success. Leadership consists of honesty, integrity, and confidence that one can overtake with time. Certain qualities that allow people to believe that people are natural born leaders could be affiliated with public speaking, confidence, responsibility, and discipline. Some people may seem to be natural born leaders compared to others; however, everyone can improve their leadership qualities and put them into a positive use every day; in and out of a workplace.

As a team, we chose to investigate, explore, and analyse the aspiring personality traits that represent a real life idea of a successful leader. These traits and characteristics are represented throughout the image of our chosen leader, Vladimir Liakhovitch. Vladimir is the General Director of Rosneft Brazil and constantly works in teams and with other people.

We conducted an interview with Vladimir on leadership has allowed a brand new perspective to be opened up on the ways one should act and behave in a professional as well as personal environment. These behaviours are designed to push and guide individuals towards working more efficiently when it comes to team projects and group affiliations.

Q: Do you consider yourself a leader? If so, why?

A: *Yes, because I enjoy leading people to success and have done it repeatedly.*

Q: Why do you think people consider you to be a leader?

A: *I am sincere, open to people and always deliver what I promise. Also, I do not give up on my goals ever.*

Q: What does leadership mean to you?

A: *Passion and results and people's trust.*

Q: How do you communicate your vision to others?

A: *Using simple and clear words spoken with sincerity, passion and unconditional commitment to reaching your goals while bringing people with you.*

Q: What was the most difficult thing you have done in your life? At work? Putting together your company?

A: *Going against the flow of prevalent thinking in the company, because you are doing what is right for the company, but not your boss. I have done it several times and it is emotionally taxing and poses a threat to your career.*

Q: What advice would you give to someone who would like to be a leader in the future?

A: *Think about people, their views and aspirations and needs, and put people's interests above everything else.*

Q: Who would you think is your best example of what it means to be a leader?

A: *I have a fundamental principle that I follow with those who report to me - any success is theirs, any failure is mine.*

Q: What was the most difficult thing you had to do with an employee/follower?

A: *Dealing with violations of the company's code of ethics.*

Q: How do you motivate people to follow you?

A: *Open my heart and mind and always, no matter what, speak the truth.*

Q: Do you think a leader needs to persuade more or listen more?

A: *Depends on the circumstances, there is not a single leadership style suited for all situations.*

Q: Is leadership about organizing people and an organization or is it about encouraging them to organize themselves?

A: *Both, depending on circumstances you may need to do both.*

Q: Have you had to create change, lead change, enforce change? How did you do it? What were the most difficult things about it?

A: *Yes, I had to transfer a company sector from a cost centre to profit centre (it was complete company sponsorship, but then had to generate income itself). Convince people that we can do it.*

Q: Is there any connection in your mind between winning and leading?

A: *Yes, but it is not linear. King Leonidas, that led 300 Spartans, ultimately suffered a defeat, but he is one of the world's greatest leaders of all time.*

Q: Do you have to be the best at anything to be a leader?

A: *Of course not! If someone is not doing a good job do you outplace them (fire them) or retrain them? You start with coaching and managing them for performance, but it can lead to release.*

Q: Do you have a different leadership/management style with different people? (Could you give some examples?)

A: *Of course, but you cannot equate leadership and management! Today people go from 6 to 12 basic leadership styles that range from "tell" to "sell."*

Q: Do you take people's personalities into account or do you treat everyone the same?

A: *Yes, we are all different and that is why the road is so amazing. Great leaders know that, and factor this into their behaviour and messages.*

Q: Do you think leaders have always been the same or that leaders now/in the future are different to the past?

A: *I think that diversity has become a cornerstone of our lives and leaders are more cognizant of this today.*

Q: What are the best/worst things about being a leader?

A: *Best - when you see your team, department, unit or company celebrating success. Worst - letting people go when times are bad.*

Q: Are you born a leader or can you learn it?

A: *I do believe that some people are born with more propensities towards leadership than others, but one can definitely acquire leadership skills through training and coaching if he/she desires it.*

Q: What are essential qualities that you think a leader needs?
A: *Integrity, authenticity, emotional intelligence, strategic thinking, ability to lead by example and work with different types of people and match leadership style to challenge at hand, sustain stress.*

Q: What are the greatest challenges in working with or managing a team?
A: *Dealing with people - their expectations, feelings and problems.*

Q: Do you think it is important to listen before speaking?
A: *Absolutely!!! Important is not really enough to emphasize how critical it is. This is the reason we have two ears and only one mouth :-)*

Q: What kind of leader do you consider yourself to be?
A: *Pragmatic, resilient, fair and passionate.*

Q: What are the most frustrating aspects of working with a team that never go away?
A: *Conflicts among people!*

Q: Do you prefer to be able to pick your team or be given a random team?
A: *I do not have a preference. Picking your own team is challenging, as you may come short on diversity of views and skills and experiences if you are driven by selecting people like yourself (as it guarantees, to an extent, a high likelihood of consensus and ease of decision-making, which is very comforting, yet ultimately wrong.)*

Q: What sort of people do you look for in a team?
A: *Different, but I absolutely require transparency in thoughts and actions from all.*

Q: When a team is functioning well, do you consider the value it brings to a project greater than one the individual effort put in?
A: *Under normal circumstances a team always delivers more than a person. However, in times of crisis, one can have greater impact than many, but it is usually limited to starting a transformation.*

Q: How do you deal with a team that is not functioning properly?
A: *Many ways - restructure and reassign tasks, provide coaching and training, introduce incentives, or disband and replace with a new one. Need to use all tools in your leadership/ management kit.*

Q: Is conflict inevitable in a team?
A: *Yes, conflict is normal; it is part of our lives. It manifests itself in different ways almost daily. We tend to overlook small ones and deal only with big ones, which ultimately means that you have failed to prevent them. Conflict prevention trumps remediation! As often said, the best fight is the one that you never had to endure.*

Q: Is there anyone that you try to avoid from adding to a team? What is this avoidable person like and why do you avoid them?

A: *People that always complain or never accept responsibility for their actions or lack of actions. One thing is to look for improvements and instigate actions and act yourself, and another one is to always complain and do nothing about it - a very toxic attitude. As adults we are responsible for what we do and do not, continuous excuses and shifting blame onto others is a no-go with me.*

Q: What role does emotion play in your decision making process?

A: *I am trying to be as unemotional as possible as I favour logical and data-driven decision-making. If I feel overwhelmed emotionally, than I physically withdraw myself from decision-making until I am fit again (emotionally balanced, calm and rational) to continue.*

Q: How do you encourage a creative and open environment within a team?

A: *By making my behavioural standards and requirements crystal clear upfront (and these include an all-inclusive environment in the team) and following through with actions including my own ones supporting such environment and offering incentives to people that promote it and disincentivising those that do not comply.*

Q: What are the most valuable lessons you have learned in being part of and managing a team?

A: *As a leader you have to have passion for your business and be resilient and open-minded and must treat people with respect. Anyone in the team can lead because leadership is not a formal position of authority - it is so much more! Top teams have a very high level of trust and performance standards, superb communication, complete commitment to stand by each other's side no matter what and an ability to recover and push through irrespectively of circumstances - effectively they achieve complete integration becoming One, like many different organs of our body.*

Besides the obvious positions within the company, (higher positions over other positions.)

Q: How do you gain respect from your teammates and not just compliance based on your position in the firm?

A: *By respecting people and their views, listening to them, opening your heart and mind to their needs, leading by example in everything you do (particularly in times of crisis), staying true to shared ethical standards, and have undeterred focus on achieving success and delivering them!*

Conclusion:

Vladimir Liakhovitch has given us an overall understanding in what leadership is and the importance on how one works with a group and or team members. Based on the interview we conducted with Vladimir, we were able to see that he is a good leader when it comes to his work because he focuses on other people's needs over his own. We have learned that there is no perfect leadership style or personality. However, there are traits that many leaders seem to exhibit such as hard work, commitment, and deeply caring about what they are doing for a specific goal or purpose they have. Furthermore, we have learned from our interview with Vladimir that people in a team are should not feel forced into working together, rather, people should feel that a team is composed of members who each possess valuable resources and each individual bring human capital to create more value than any individual alone. Leadership and being a part of a team is about gaining more than one could by him or her while working towards a clear common goal that all members must care about.

5

Building Teams

No man will make a great leader who wants to do it all himself or get all the credit for doing it.

Andrew Carnegie

Discipline of teams

Back in 1993 Jon Katzenback and Douglas Smith published an article in the HBR called 'The Discipline of Teams.' In that article they defined teams as "a small number of people with complementary skills who are committed to a common purpose, a set of performance goals and approach for which they hold themselves mutually accountable".

A leader may be someone who runs an organization of thousands of people but chances are that one of the key things that makes them effective is their ability to form a strong team around them.

In this chapter we are going to look at the nature of that team. The idea of the 'common purpose' has already been touched off in the section of this book dedicated to Vision (and will also be looked at in the section on Motivation). There is a separate chapter on performance goals and holding people mutually accountable is dealt with both hear and the chapter on 'Doing the Hard Things.

Some of the values that Katzenback and Smith talk about in relation to a team is the need to have an environment of listening, responding constructively to one another's ideas, giving people the benefit of the doubt, supporting each other and recognizing other people's interests and individual and group achievements.

It is also important to point out that the team should have a purpose which is aligned with but not the same as the Vision of the overall organisation. And the team should spend plenty of time making sure that they are clear on and are happy with that purpose, as it will give direction, meaning and motivation to the team the same way that a larger Vision will motivate the entire organisation.

One of the ideas that I like about this article – which seems obvious but oftentimes is not, and leads to a lot of resentment – is that everyone should have equivalent amounts of real work. This means that while everyone might be doing different jobs and tasks, the feeling is that everyone is doing the same amount of work. Real work means that people are not just given tasks to keep them busy but are doing things that have real value.

Dysfunctions of a Team

In 2002 Lencioni talked about different dysfunctions of a team and how to overcome those dysfunctions.[19] Two of these dysfunctions are 'a fear of conflict' and 'a lack of trust'. The three other areas, Lack of Commitment, Accountability and Inattention to results are covered elsewhere.

A lack of trust means that people do not share with other others on the team, do not ask for or give feedback and try to undermine each other. A leader therefore will have to promote an atmosphere where people can be vulnerable around each other, admit mistakes in a healthy environment, and have an overarching vision for the group that people can sign up to.

The fear of conflict is another key dysfunction. Some teams can appear to be happy on the surface. No-one argues with anyone else or criticizes others. There is no conflict at any of the team meetings. The problem is that people leave unresolved differences off the table and never push forward with hard but necessary decisions. A false consensus makes meetings boring and very often leads to negative gossip and backstabbing away from the team meetings. It may also mean GroupThink[20] happens. This is where conformity to the group

---

[19] "5 Dysfunctions of a Team" by Patrick Lencioni is written like a story for most of the book about a woman who takes over a board of directors of a company and then forges them into a team. The lessons are clear and there is a section at the end where the main ideas are laid out clearly.

[20] The idea of GroupThink was originally introduced by Irving Janis in 1970 and can be used to describe the negative effects of ingroup

and its norms and the creation of an in-group often leads to irrational decisions being taken that are a complete disaster when they leave the "safe" confines of the group itself.

To overcome this, trust has to be built by the leader and critical thinking, open debate and criticism has to be encouraged. I should point out that bringing conflict to the table does not mean personal attacks which should NOT be brought to team meetings. This is about constructive criticism, feedback and getting potentially difficult topics on the table where they are dealt with honestly[21].

It might be necessary for the leader to help the team members become more confident and assertive in this area and to act as a mediator at times.

Belbin's Team Roles

---

behaviour in teams ranging from Governments to a high school group of friends.

[21] In Tuckman's five stages of a team, he identifies two stages that are relevant here. The first is forming where everyone comes together and are polite towards each other at the beginning, but everyone puts their own interests first. The second stage is storming which is often a necessary stage (though some teams successfully avoid it) where the leader's authority is challenged, differences are aired, norms begin to develop around the functioning of the team etc. When this stage of conflict is viewed as a natural process of getting towards a high performance team, and this process is explained to the team, then conflict can be viewed as something positive rather than negative.

The final area we are going to look at in the area of Teams are the roles that Team members play. Specifically we are going to look at Belbin's Team Roles. In the 1970s Meredith Belbin was looking at high performance teams – called Apollo teams, which had the "best" performers in each area working together. What he found was that these Apollo teams were not always the most successful. On many occasions the sum of the parts was less than the parts on their own. On the hand some of the highest performing teams were made up of diverse individuals who on their own would not have been considered the highest performers in the company. In these case the sum of the parts was much greater than the parts on their own.

Belbin identified 9 (originally 8) key roles that a high performance team needed. While it is possible that an individual can play several roles, the roles themselves are necessary.

These are divided into three main groups – People, Thought and Action Roles. In the People roles, resource investigators are enthusiastic 'liaison' members who deal with other people outside the group and bring resources from outside into the group. The Team Worker is the Glue that holds the group together and the coordinator is the person who focuses and organises the team (often aligned with the traditional view of what a leader is).

The Thought Roles involve the Plant – the creative member of the team, the critical thinking Monitor Evaluators, and the

Specialists who are, as the names suggests, experts in a particular area.

Finally the Action Roles include the Shaper who motivates and challenges people to improve, the Implementer who ensures that things get done and the Completer Finisher who keeps an eye on details and deadlines.

All of these roles are important (as opposed to specific people) and rather than focusing on how personalities work together this model aims at ensuring that every team has the right functions for optimal performance.

Key Takeaways

1. A team needs a common purpose
2. A team needs to have a climate of trust where people feel safe to express their ideas and are given the benefit of the doubt.
3. A team needs to hold themselves mutually accountable.
4. Everyone has to do equal amounts of real work.
5. Constructive conflict is a good thing in a team.
6. There are different roles on a team that have to be taken into account to ensure the team performs properly. Dividing up the roles with foresight and ensuring that different people take care of different roles means that the team as a whole will be more effective.

6

𝒯he 𝒮tork

𝒜 leader creates leaders

Manuela Viéytez

Andrea Trevison

Eduardo Troncoso

Abigail Woermann

"The Red Pandas"

PART I: Defining the Project

1. Finding a vision

When a group is first created, if there is one thing that must be
done before starting to work or even think about a project, it

is to make sure that everyone is on the same page and that all minds of the group will put their efforts towards achieving a common goal. This is why our first goal as a group was to create a vision which represented all of us. One with which we all agreed and by which we were motivated. After giving it some hard thought, we came up with the following sentence: "Our group aims to act as an integrated and collaborative workforce, in which everyone's joint efforts, inspiration and ideas will open the door to not only successful work results, but also a combined feeling of gratification and a development of each of our individual leadership styles." After this was set in stone, it became easy to work together: we all added strength to the group.

2.   Who (or what!) is our leader?

Our first important debate as a group was choosing a leader that was worth showcasing and that inspired each of us. We decided to select ***The Stork***, IE University's Official Newspaper, which we initially chose because of its entrepreneurial spirit. Furthermore, we felt that the way in which they are breaking barriers at university by expressing constructive criticism of some taboo topics is inspiring. In addition, most of us personally knew the founder, the young and extremely talented Volodymyr Lakomov and some of us even work at The Stork, so there also a personal incentive to choose the organization.

3. Why is Stork a leader?

As time went on and our research and contact with The Stork deepened, we came to the realization that there were many more reasons why it could be considered a leader organization and that leadership is more than just what meets the eye, since it was also hidden in the consequences of the work done by the newspaper. This can be exemplified by the simple fact that they have taken action on giving the students a voice. We believe that putting the spotlight or showing a new side to IE community members who previously did not have the recognition they deserve, such as some staff members or professors, is also a way of leading.

Other reasons include the fact that that the organization is well run and motivated. They inspire students to speak their minds openly and have great growth aspirations with smart goals, which they are constantly working towards. Last but not least, the people who work there have become a community, instead of being just another group of co-workers.

4. How can we show it is a leader?

So, after realizing and acknowledging all the aforementioned reasons which explain why The Stork is in fact a leader organization in our eyes, we brainstormed a way in which we could show it. While getting insights from the founder was interesting, we as a group knew that all the efforts and rewards must not belong solely to one person. This is why we took the decision to focus our project on the founder, but also on all those around him. By showcasing how the students, who worked alongside the founder and helped the organization grow, were also leaders, we could more justly show that a top organization is born from the hands and brains of many.

Once we had decided this, it was a manner of how and in which platform to bring our project to life. After much negotiation, we decided to create a LinkedIn campaign, which would brand The Stork as a leadership example by showing how many of their workers and how the people who ultimately give life to the newspapers, were themselves leaders. Perhaps they were so in different categories and through different actions, but leaders nonetheless.

Part II: The Stork LinkedIn Leadership Campaign

1. Main Goal:
Showcase The Stork as a leader organization in the realm of student led newspapers.

2. Background:
The Stork is "a project founded to create a platform for IEU's voices to deliver compelling stories that would inform, inspire, and entertain the IE Community as well as help IE's mission in bridging its community." A place to express and share thoughts, ideas and passions, a place where the student's experience can be improved through information.

3. The Stork's vision:
"Aspire to create a platform for IEU's voices to be heard on the international arena and to be recognized as a source of leading and influential academic opinion."

4. The Stork's mission is found in 4 statements.
i. To provide practical journalistic experience to IE University students.
ii. To provide an open forum to members of the university community for an exchange of ideas and opinions.
iii. To report and comment on news and issues pertinent to the university community in accordance with and professional journalistic practice and ethics.
iv. To publish creative and entertaining essays, reviews, feature stories, artwork, and other editorial matter of interest to the university community.

Following the organization's mission, we could define the target audience in order to create and craft posts that are noticeable and relevant for the ideal audience.

5. Target Audience:
Firstly, IE University Students and Professors. This is especially important because some IE University students and professors still don't know, or know little about the organization. The people who are still unaware of the newspaper, could be

reached out through LinkedIn. At the same time, we aim to demonstrate The Stork to be a leader organization within the IE community.

Another one of our desired target audience are business people and newspaper owners. We aim to reach them because it is important to expand The Stork's presence and leadership among Spanish, American and British newspapers. Also, we consider that some of our desired target audience can be called the 'Inspiration Seekers', which can be either part of the IE or the newspaper related community, or not. Why not be a source of inspiration for those who want to be entrepreneurs? We want to inspire those who 'bump into' or are already following The Stork's LinkedIn and demonstrate to them that it is a leader organization.

Even though The Stork has already used its LinkedIn to publish their stories and most important articles, we want our posts to be different. Then, we came up with a strategy which could aid us in making our posts unique and stand out from the rest.

6. Statement and differentiation:
#StoriesNotBabies:

The official "hashtag" of the LinkedIn campaign. We are aware that you can't use hashtags when posting on LinkedIn. Then we decided the slogan is our inspiration for our posts. How? We are delivering the leadership stories (and not the babies) of a lot of people who work in the organization. And since this is the official organization's slogan, for which it is perfect to better identify The Stork.

7. Creating Leaders:

Our other inspiration comes from the quote "True leaders don't create followers, they create more leaders": The main aim of the campaign is for The Stork to be known as a leader organization, but also showcasing the people inside the organization, not only the Editor in Chief as a leader, but also the other editors, the social media manager and the writers. We want to showcase their stories on how they have become leaders through their job at The Stork. To these leaders, The Stork might have been a platform, an aid, an inspiration, etc. when becoming leaders.

But to go even further, to inspire others and to reach our target audience, we decided to create our specific "post reader", who we know for sure, he would be personally engaged by our posts.

8. Buyer Persona (understanding others):

This person is a Dreamer and aspirer who seeks the good in other people and feels inspired by others stories. They want to be informed about what is happening around their community. Sometimes they might be considered a workaholic, always working to achieve their great goals for their future. Nevertheless they are positive, yet could be a pessimist sometimes by thinking most people are not making a positive impact in the world. Always with an entrepreneurial spirit, wants to become a 21st century business person.

9. Goal setting:

Having all these designed it is crucial to have our main aim or objectives written down. First, we considered that we wanted to demonstrate The Stork as a leader organization by showcasing the members of the organization. Then if possible we wanted to share current and previous articles that help reach our goals. Last but not least, we wish to demonstrate key metrics and growth.

But to demonstrate these key metrics and growth, we determined specific key performance indicators. Our first one is that we aim for a Post reach: 25+ people. We strive to Grow followers on LinkedIn. And an essential key performance indicator would be that when someone is asked about The Stork, they can mention leadership attributes.

10. Vision:

Through this marketing plan we aim to aid The Stork in attracting a bigger market, but also in rebranding the way in which people see them, so that everyone can look at the newspaper and think of leadership, in the way that we now do. We strongly believe that bringing a newspaper up from zero shows great ambition and passion, especially so when it is done by students. We hope that through this campaign we will manage to give the newspaper and its team members the recognition they deserve.

Part III: Meet the Team

As we mentioned, The Stork has many great leaders and we wish to inspire you through their stories.

1. Volodymyr Lakomov

"The Stork transmits IE's culture and vision to the world." He is the Founder and Editor in Chief of the Stork. Originally from Ukraine, he has lived in Pakistan, Brazil and Spain, which allowed him to gain unique notions and a diverse perspective on cultures since a very young age. He is extremely interested in investigatory journalism and world events. This interest grew especially through an internship he had on a local newspaper in Namibia. Today he is the leader at the Stork, which has given him organizational and professional skills. He sees a future for himself in the management of companies, even maybe his own. His genius lies in creating a vision it, sharing it, transmitting it and inspiring others to come with him on the journey.

2. Adriana Rodríguez Rivera: This powerful lady is the current Editor in Chief of the Stork for the Madrid Campus. Originally from Madrid, she has lived in Beijing and went to an international school there. This experience allowed her to work with students from all nationalities, hence giving her a better perspective on multiculturalism and its benefits for innovation and progress. Her interest in international relations and comparative law became clear when living in Beijing. After 3

years of studying this, she has become attracted to writing and politics. She aims at getting involved in a political think tank, as well as working in the Spanish legislature. As the leader of the Stork, she has learned to put a business plan model like the Stork into practice and successfully overcome the difficult obstacles that may arise. She is a coordinator and an implementer.

3. Nicolás López

He is the next editor in-chief for IE University Madrid Campus. Nicolás was born in Quito and raised in Guayaquil. Since young, he developed a passion for writing, which took him to recently write his first fictional novel titled "Law of the Jungle". Previous to becoming the new Editor in Chief, he worked at The Stork as a news editor. He currently studies Business Administration, in the hope of becoming an entrepreneur and running his own business one day. He is also currently working on his own start-up application named "Baits", a digital flyer platform. Nico's friendliness, positive attitude, and talent are recognised by the whole team, which is what made him be selected for the head position. We are excited to see how he handles this position and his future career. He is the glue and the inspiration for the team.

4. Matt Lawson

He is the future editor and chief for Segovia Campus IE Stork. Matt, 20 years old, comes from a very diverse background. He was born in Scotland from a Swiss Argentine mother and a Zambian born father, and he has lived most of his live in Portugal. Furthermore he is well travelled and hopes to continue exploring and learning about new cultures. As well as being very open-minded, Matt is also very attentive. He takes a lot of pride in his work. Additionally he believes that his endeavours in life should never come at the expense of others and rather he hopes to follow a career path that betters society. He maintains that he still has a long way to go to achieve his dreams. However he feels that he has been able to develop vital skills in leadership such as listening, respecting different perspectives, facilitating discussion and organizational skills. "I don´t think I've always been a natural leader, but I have been able to develop my leadership skills and grow."

5. Manuela Viéytez

Manuela Vieytez was born and raised in El Salvador. One of her favourite hobbies is dancing, she studied jazz, tap and ballet during her childhood years, and even competed at an international level on the Dance Educator's of America competition. She was also attracted to the media and journalism, which led her to be a social media influential figure in the blogging area. She created her own restaurant reviews food blog in El Salvador, which gave her a first-hand opportunity with media relations. Then, her interest for the field influenced her decision to become a bachelor in digital media and communications student and The Stork's first official Sports Editor. Soon she will be taking on the role of Spanish Editor and will be not only in charge of copy editing the Storks Spanish section, but in charge of the expansion of the newspaper in the Spanish territory. At The Stork, Manuela has learned about Team Management and has had the opportunity to apply different skills and virtues that she will continue using during her career as a journalist.

6. Lupita Prada

Lupita is a passionate, independent and determined woman, born in Medellin, Colombia. Since a very young age, she started to participate in the Model United Nations, where she developed her passion for diplomacy and Latin America. She graduated school having participated in over 25 MUN conferences, and was even appointed by the major of her city and governor of state city as the Secretary General of her State's MUN which hosted over 1000 students. She is currently studying Law and International Relations, and after several working experiences, including one in the Organization of American States, she is decided to pursue diplomacy in her future. Lupita has also an interest in journalism, especially concerning politics and opinion, which led her to become the Opinion Editor of The Stork. She has written for both this newspaper and also has her own opinion blog called The

Global View. She hopes to become an important facilitator of Latin American integration to the International Community, through the use of diplomacy and potentially, journalism.

7. Andrea Trevisan

She was born and raised in Venezuela, she studied at the German school of Caracas, where she learnt German and English. After successfully completing her ABI diploma, moved to Segovia to study communications. Today she holds the first place of her class and is also Class Representative, an honour at IE. Also, since a young age she developed a love for volleyball, which led her to become the IE Volleyball Team captain, and a sports writer at The Stork. After being in charge of the mental health writing department, she was just selected to become the new Sports Editor for the Segovia for 2019. At The Stork she learnt about responsibility, by creating a by-weekly mental health related post. She also implemented and improved certain communication skills, such as pitching and copy-writing.

Working with The Stork has been a great experience for us. We have learned about creating a vision together, bringing together diverse views of the world and life experiences. We have shown how different personalities, and different roles for each person, can make the whole team even stronger. Inspired by Volodymyr Lakomov we all feel like leaders, that we all make up The Stork, and that while we deliver stories and not babies, we do feel that the newspaper itself is our baby. Now that we think of it, does that make Volodymyr a Level 5 leader without us realising it? We hope that learning about these young people has inspired you, because university students can also be entrepreneurs and leaders.

7

Motivation

The art of making problems so interesting and their solutions so constructive that everyone wants to get to work and deal with them.

Paul Hawken

When it comes to being a leader, you might be able to create a vision that everyone understands, you might even understand the people who are following you. But as Anthony Robbins says 'what differentiates those go succeed from those who don't is action.'[22] Motivation has its origin in the concept of 'movement' and that's what is key here, not simply convincing people about the merits of your vision but also getting them to act on it.

Instinct and Drive Theories

These revolve around the idea that people are motivated by internal drives. Going back to the 1930s Mc Dougall covered

---

[22] The performance and personal success coach Anthony Robbins has written several books and positively influenced millions of people. I suggest you start with his book "Unlimited Power" (which also gives some great practical tips on how to apply NLP with yourself and others).

17 instincts – covering areas such as 'laughter' and escape. William James later focused on 37 instincts such as "cleanliness", "fear of dark places" and "smiling". By treating people as a collective of instinctual responses, motivation here almost becomes manipulation, like treating everyone like a more intelligent Pavlov's dog.

More recently Steven Reiss introduced the idea of 16 desires. These are: Power, Independence, Curiosity, Acceptance, Order, Saving, Honour, Idealism, Social contact, Family, Status, Vengeance, Romance, Eating, Physical exercise and tranquillity.

The belief here is by understand what people desire you can motivate them better by taking this into account. If people are strongly motivated by independence then they should be allowed more freedom at work (within their capabilities and the requirements of the job) to choose when to arrive at work or when to leave, for example. If they are more motivated by tranquillity, order and family then asking them regularly at the last minute to work until late into the night might not be the best way to maintain their levels of motivation.

Mc Gregor's Theory X and Theory Y

These twin theories reflect different ways of looking at how and why people work and their dual division is reflected in many theories of Leadership that divide leadership styles into ones that are more focused on the task or more focused on people.

Theory X views workers as being untrustworthy, unambitious, lazy, resistant to change and motivated by money.   With a view of workers like this then it is necessary to introduce a system of external rewards and punishments to get people to work and ensure strong processes and systems of control.

Theory Y supposes that people are motivated by doing a job well, that they want to take on responsibility, want to grow in the job and are happy to be experience change and use creativity at work.

These two different perceptions of how people approach work are intimately linked to many of the other ideas of how to motivate people.   Abraham Maslow's famous hierarchy of needs says that at the bottom of the pyramid people are motivated by food and shelter and then when they have these needs met they gradually move up through the different layers (shelter, social contact, etc.) to self-actualization, doing something that they find fulfilling.

Herzberg's Hygiene Factors

Herzberg looks at some of the elements of Theory X and Theory Y and says they are indeed relevant for employees and followers – people do want a good salary, good working conditions, and a decent timetable.   However, he calls many of these factors 'Hygiene factors'.   That means that if people do not have them they will be dissatisfied with their job, unhappy with the work conditions and will do badly. However, if they have these elements they will not be motivated to work harder – it is as if these are the minimum needed to get them to do the minimum.

Motivators are more connected with the self-actualization of Maslow, getting recognition for a job done well, greater responsibility and advancement on the job.

Drive

Daniel Pink[23] has taken many of these ideas and put them into three key ways of motivating people in the 21st Century:

- Autonomy
- Mastery
- Purpose

Pink believes that to feel truly motivated by the job their doing people need autonomy over the task they are doing, the team they are doing it with, the time they have to do it with and the technique they use to carry it out. In this case the leader's role is to define what the overall direction is (the Commander's intent mentioned in the chapter on vision) but the means to get there is in the hands of the trusted followers.

Mastery refers to the fact that followers are given objectives that 'stretch' them. Not so impossible that they give up but just difficult enough to make them strive to improve. The Leader has to develop a certain mind-set in their followers that they can constantly improve, constantly do something

---

[23] I am a big fan of Daniel Pink and how he writes. I believes he takes complex ideas and reduces them to easy to understand and apply concepts. If you are interested in a book on Motivation I strongly recommend that you start with Drive.

better, always get closer to perfection – without ever completely reaching it.

The final key element to Pink's theory of motivation is Purpose. People need to feel that their work matters more than just to themselves. What they are doing is more than just a pay check, and that they belong to a company or organisation that is about more than profit maximisation. This is where the leader's ability to create an inspiring vision for their followers comes into play.

Some Key Ideas

1. Knowing what to do is not the same as actually doing it.
2. Doing it is not the same as wanting to do it.
3. People are motivated by more than money.
4. A leader has to trust their followers to be the type of people who want to work – if not they are more like control managers than leaders.
5. It IS necessary to have good pay, working conditions etc. but not to motivate people. These simply stop people from being unhappy at work.
6. Create an inspiring purpose to work as this is one of the best motivators.

8

Maria Eizaguirre: "True Leaders Transmit Passion"

Giulia Camargo

Even though leadership is unique to us all, every great leader has one thing in common; flexibility. The ability to mold their approaches to fit the situation is something crucial in being an effective leader. Maria Eizaguirre, the founding marketing director of IE University for five years, personifies a successful example of real leadership - humble, empathetic and passionate.

Eizaguirre obtained her bachelor's degree in Anthropology. She started her career in consumer insights and behavior, first at a research agency (Research International), followed by an advertising agency (Young & Rubicam) and for the last eight years at Kraft Foods within the Consumer Insights & Strategy team, where she was leading the Innovation CI function across the EU and is currently Director Insights and Innovation for IE University. Her primary interest is in the use of Anthropology as a tool to understand and interpret consumer behavior and her extensive research on human societies, cultures and their development set a foundation for her becoming a successful leader, due to her ability to understand people's motivations and be able to inspire them to give their best allowed her to be considered a leader in every sense of the word.

1. "Through connecting with who I am, I can inspire different types of people"

However, Eizaguirre doesn't consider herself to be a leader. She has "realized with time that I speak from the heart and put all my effort and passion into all initiatives, and this attitude helps me to lead better. I am empathetic, creative and curious and think this helps me adjust to many different situations." Maria shows how true leadership is humble; it is about how other people view you, not how one views oneself. Leadership is about being modest and transmitting a passion and desire to do the right thing. Nevertheless, in order to set a foundation, the leader must embody certain personality traits to lead better. In the interview, Maria also stated that she "found that following a true vocation helps me lead myself better and through connecting with who I am, I can inspire different types of people in the spheres of acting in which I work" showing that leadership is also about engaging and helping people engage in causes bigger than oneself, in order to find true self-fulfillment.

Maria is the embodiment of a transformational leader, as she strongly believes people must always be motivated. She thinks that we chose her as our leadership example because we "value this passion that [she] is talking about, someone with experience who is capable of transmitting that experience." Maria considers the transmission of knowledge in a clear and effective way to be extremely important, as communication is the foundation to a structured organization. In order to achieve success, people must believe in their leader's values.

2. "There was no heart at all. It destroyed me as a person."

Eizaguirre also explains the dangers of working for a leader whose values, passion or goals don't align with your own. The most difficult thing she had to do in her life at work "was to accept a job in a company whose culture was radically different to who I am as a person. [She] spent a year seeing live the consequences of that decision. It was a company that stood for selfishness, individuality, foul play, which was focused on form rather than content and completely oriented to numbers. There was no heart at all. It destroyed me as a person." This is a concrete example of the difference between leaders and managers and shows how uninspiring managers create dissonance within their followers, and instead of focusing on doing the correct thing, they are more focused on doing things correctly, and their ultimate goal will always be money.

3. "Believe in what you are doing and believe in people and their concerns."

Furthermore, it is important to understand that there is not one correct type of leader. Leadership depends on situation and prediction, for example, is people-oriented vs. being task oriented will be more effective depending on the context one is leading within. A piece of advice Maria gave to all future leaders was to "believe in what you are doing and believe in people and their concerns. Don't rush things, be proactive, and show initiative. Have your point of view but be sensible in the way you propose things, and always try and add your own "twist" to things. Try to read situations carefully before you act, but don't plan too much. And above all, don't try to show off - arrogance and speed are the killers for a person."

The only common thread between the way all successful leaders work should be their strong belief, proactive nature and originality. If a leader leads from the 'why' and knows the world is a better place with their presence, they will be able to inspire others to believe as well. Proactivity and originality are also important when inspiring people, as one is more likely to follow a leader who is constantly reinventing what is considered normal, and that's what Maria Eizaguirre does, by always adding her "own twist" to everything she does.

An example of a leader for María is someone that embodies all her most important traits is Malala Yousafzai. She describes her leadership as holding "feminine values" And exemplifies "vocation, knowing what she stands for, and speaking from the heart, with authenticity and passion" leading María, of course, to believe in her cause. This is because the first step to driving change is inspiring your followers to do the same.

4. "Standing for what you think is right always makes you enemies"

María Eizaguirre has also been at the forefront of creating and leading change in IE University. She "created, almost from scratch, a way of working that was completely different to what was common at the time." This was difficult and made her a lot of enemies as not everyone sees change and progress as a good thing, especially when it makes others obsolete. "Standing for what you think is right always makes you enemies" she states. Being a leader is not about having everyone like you, it's about doing what you believe is right and sticking by it, and as Winston Churchill once said, "If you have enemies, good - it means you have stood up for something in this life" and people will respect you for that.

5. "Be ready to find creative solutions to blocked doors"

Being a leader also takes stamina, creativity and a lot of political savviness. "Be ready to find creative solutions to blocked doors, this doesn't mean bumping your head against a rubber wall, but if you see an obstacle, always look for ways around it." Leaders must know how to understand people's needs and motivations and put them at the forefront of change, by letting others lead, they are more likely to assimilate your beliefs as their own. Eizaguirre states "I believe too much in human beings. Enforcement is never the way."

6. "If you don't make space for empathy, you cannot lead"

According to Maria Eizaguirre's leadership style, it all starts with the person. She believes that "if you don't make space for empathy, you cannot lead. If you don't make way to understand where someone is speaking from you have no chance at all to lead anything at all." Nowadays, there are many technologies that can help us understand people better, whether it be testing for personality types with the 16 Personalities Quiz or using Crystal to analyze people's LinkedIn profiles, we have no excuse for not attempting to understand people's wants before allocating them specific tasks. I believe that most problems are caused by not knowing how to deal with different personality types, as arguments can be avoided if everyone took a personality test first!

7. "How can you progress if you keep your head down?"

Furthermore, being objective is another important trait in a successful leader. Eizaguirre mentions that "the most difficult thing [she] had to do with an employee was promoting someone in [her] team who [she] disliked strongly as a person, instead of promoting someone who "worked liked [her]." On very few occasions, a leader must look past personality traits and focus on the bigger picture. If a person, despite your views their personality, is the most qualified for the job, hiring them would be the best solution. Nevertheless, it is always important to weigh if their personality is a crucial aspect of the type of job they will be required to do. On the other hand, with students, Eizaguirre finds it most difficult to "work with disinterest, with open computers and eyes down." She generally finds it hard to work with people (students or employees) who "don't "look up" and constantly asks herself "how can you progress if you keep your head down?" but overcoming these types of struggles, is what makes a good leader.

8. "If you start leading yourself, you have a better chance to lead others."

The interview with our leader Maria Eizaguirre concluded with an age-old question: Are you born a leader, or do you become one? To which she intelligently answered: "I think you have to be born with a passion for human beings and a curiosity to learn. But empathy, creativity can be learned and improved. And age helps a lot to accept who you are. If you start leading yourself, you have a better chance to lead others. And that, you can learn." As we can see, a healthy mixture of traits such as interest, passion, and curiosity, which reside within every human at birth, need to be fostered and developed to form a successful leader. No one is born knowing how to lead, but the ones who are born with a natural interest in people are more likely to succeed in the challenging task.

9

Communication

Leadership is a way of thinking, a way of acting and, most importantly, a way of communicating.

Simon Sinek

One of the key abilities of a leader is an ability to communicate effectively. I would argue, and I am not alone, that communicating does not start with speaking, it starts with listening.

Listening

The first step you have to take with listening is not even the other person, it is you, developing a listening frame of mind. That means *wanting* to hear what the other person says. Expect to find it interesting and more often than not, it will be, simply because you have changed your perspective from you, to them.

I did not like show jumping, I am still not a huge fan, but recently I had to listen to a presentation precisely on this subject. I could have decided, like some of the other people in the audience, that show jumping was not a sport I was particularly into and like them, switched off immediately.

However, on the basis that if I teach it I should practice it, I decided to adopt a Listening frame of mind. That meant instead of deciding whether the information I was hearing was good or bad, or whether I agreed with it or not, or whether it was useful or useless, I decided that I was interested. That was the only change. And the presentation was fascinating. I learned so much – including the fact that I am not getting my children interested in one of the most dangerous, expensive sports on the planet!

There is a tendency for most of us, myself included, to listen to others with one ear, the other ear is turned inwards, listening to what we are thinking about saying as soon as the other person finishes talking. We have an internal commentary running, filtering what they are saying through our opinions, plans, possible interjections and biases.

In the Western system of education, going back to the Greeks, we are often thought how to refute what the other person is saying, to prove that we are right and they are wrong. Instead of this, as a leader we have to start from a position of learning to understand.

When we have adopted a listening frame of mind we can then move onto the specific techniques of deep listening.

Reducing questions to a minimum: instead of asking questions (whether they be open or closed), which are good to get the conversation going and for drilling down in specific areas, try echoing, repetition and minimal encouragers. When you echo and repeat you identify key words the other person says and repeat them. The key words that they use will often be words related to emotions ("I was really upset when X happened", "Upset", "Yeah, I didn't expect.....") and qualifiers such as "really, incredibly, terribly". Minimal encourager include 'hmm', 'aha', etc.

Visual keys: Show that you are listening by matching their body language, nodding your head (when that is what the culture of the speaker does) and adopting open, receptive body language. Focus on being there in the moment so that you are not just listening, the other person *knows* you are listening. Otherwise you are simply receiving information and listening is in fact two-way communication.

Mirroring & Pacing

In NLP[24] one of the techniques used to create rapport with the other side is to mirror them. This has several levels. First of all it means adopting similar body language to their – leaning forward/backwards with them, slow/fast movements, expansive/limited gestures. This helps you to get in sync with them. Do not copy them exactly or they will realise this and, normally, react defensively.

---

[24] "Introducing NLP" by Joseph O'Connor and John Seymour is a comprehensive study of the subject. NLP's heyday is certainly over, but so many of its techniques are still applicable and will help you as a leader, presenter and communicator

You can also match the **prosody** of their speech – speak faster if they do, louder or softer, with greater or lesser intensity. A number of years ago I found myself in a situation where I had to get a mother who was very hysterical to calm down. She was shouting and upset about a situation she was going through at the time with her son. I was trying to elicit information from her by phone but could not get her to listen to me. What I had to do was raise my voice substantially and fill it with the same intensity of emotion as hers. At that point we were in synch and I was able to quickly reduce the volume, intensity and speed of my speech. She followed me down and I was able to get the information from her that I needed to resolve the situation.

One last area of NLP is the concept of **representational systems** – how we represent the world internally. According to NLP there are four main representational systems[25].

1. Visual
2. Auditory
3. Kinaesthetic
4. Auditory Digital (inner dialogue/self-talk

(There are also gustatory (taste) and olfactory (smell) but if they are used they are normally grouped with Kinaesthetic).

---

[25] This classification is taken from the accessible and reader friendly book "NLP in 21 Days" by Harry Adler and Beryl Heather.

People who are primarily Visual 'see' the world and when they speak they have a tendency to use words and phrases such as 'I see your point', 'Look at this point', 'I'll see you next week.'

People who are prefer an auditory system can remember what others said and can even hear their voices in their head. You can tell these people when they communicate because they use expressions like 'I hear what you say', 'I'll speak to you next week', 'That rings a bell.'

Kinaesthetic people perceive the world internally in terms of touch, pressure, how things feel and experiencing things physically. They use language like 'we'll be in touch' or 'I'd like to feel out that idea first.'

Auditory digital people use words from all the rest but also more abstract language like 'conceive', 'understand', 'think' etc.

By listening to the way people communicate it also gives you an idea of how to communicate with them. This way people feel that 'you get them'. It also means that instead of a visual person having to translate the auditory and kinaesthetic communication style you are using into more appropriate for them 'visual language' and images, that they process the pictures you present them with immediately.

If you are presenting your vision to an audience you should combine all the styles and repeat your key ideas in different ways to increase the probability that it will resonate with them.

Speaking

Communicate clearly by using some of the following simple techniques:

Labelling: Tell them what you are doing. 'I'm going to summarise some of the main ideas now.' 'I'd like to ask you a question.' 'I want to focus on the main idea of our conversation now.' By literally telling people what to do in the conversation you reduce the bandwidth that they use up trying to understand the structure of your conversation.

Speak in terms of their interests: Regularly use expressions like 'You'll find this interesting', or 'It's important that you remember this...' or 'this will really help you in future.'

Clear language: Indirect, high context language is very common in certain cultures. However, unless you are trying to be deliberately vague, this does not help communication of Vision, goal setting and giving feedback.   Sometimes it helps to give summaries of what you have just said. This way you also force yourself to speak in a way that others will remember.

Check understanding: Rather than asking people 'Do you understand?' ask them to tell you what they have understood. This may seem like you are treating them like children but you can introduce the request in a self-defacing way such as 'Sometimes I overly complicate things. Would you mind repeating back to me what you have understood just so I can be sure I've covered all the main points.'

Include them in the conversation: If you find that you have been speaking for five minutes without any interaction from them, then you have lost them.   Get them involved and concentrating on what you are saying, even with something as simple as a question tag 'We're going to focus on increasing production on line 5, right?' If you overuse this technique it may sound like you are not sure of yourself but it does get constant agreement and attention from the listener. Other ways of getting them involved is asking for their opinion, for questions, for suggestions about how to implement different ideas. You will find that this slows down conversations a lot and is not useful for urgent situations. However it is much better for engagement and memory recall.

*

Later we will look at some of the techniques of persuasion in more detail in its own chapter.

Key Takeaways

1. Adopt a listening frame of mind
2. Reduce direct questions through the use of echoing and minimal encouragers.
3. Look like your listening, as opposed to just listening.
4. Use mirroring and pacing to create rapport (in prosody, body language and actual language used)
5. Understand the different representational systems that exist in NLP
6. Use labelling techniques to make your message clear.
7. Check understanding
8. Include them in the conversation.

10

Madhumita Das

Giving back

Daniel Padilla

Beatriz Rodríguez

María Oar

Juan Carlos Muñoz

Ana Nieto

10 Lessons We Learned About Leadership

1. What does leadership mean for us after this project?

It is not very early in our lives that we start hearing about the concept of leadership; however, we are exposed to it from the very beginning. Think about it, when your mum was giving birth to you, the whole situation was being led by a doctor, who worked in a team with nurses and other staff members. People tend to think that the figure of the doctor (leader) could carry out the whole procedure by themselves, not needing the role of the others. Yet if the doctor had to take care of every single detail, it would be very likely that something would go wrong. This is our main "take-away": a leader is an important figure, but just as important are the leader's followers and peers. At the end of the day, the most important factor is how well these people work together - and that task is the leader's responsibility.

2. Ability to Listen

Firstly, one of the main things that should characterize a leader's personality is the ability to listen and value everyone's opinion. Apart from being a good communicator, a leader must respect the people they work with; otherwise they will never be respected. How? A leader must listen, accept and give proper reasons when taking a decision. This is not only a sign of esteem, but also a way of motivating others to engage with the project. At the end of the day, people always like to work on their ideas, as it provides them with a feeling of realisation and self-esteem; and if they do not do so, they want (and must) understand *why*.

3. Ability to Communicate

Second, a leader must have the ability to communicate. They could have great ideas, but, as mentioned before, will never succeed by themselves alone. When working in groups, a leader should be tolerant enough to incorporate every good idea into the project, regardless of who proposed it; personal egos have killed thousands of good ideas. And even if they do not perceive this as the best way, sometimes it is better to give in rather than creating conflict or discomfort. These circumstances must be seen as simple negotiations, it works the same way.

4. Identifying people's personalities, potential and responsibilities

Something indispensable when performing a leader role is identifying the various characters and personality types they are working with. Not only must a leader complete their part of the job, but also recognize people's potential and assign them appropriate tasks respectively. In order to motivate someone to fulfil a certain task, the followers must either like it or be good at it (most of times this two terms come together, or are highly correlated). This sometimes may incur assigning yourself something you might not like the most, but no one said being the leader would always be beneficial for oneself.

All the same, let's not forget that a leader should not only please their colleagues, but also focus on their obligations and make sure everyone complies with theirs. A leader must be organised and data-focused, always foreseeing any possible unexpected events. When something does not come out the way it was expected, it is the leader's duty to guarantee that it will be fixed; for example, the damage caused by a free rider.

Nevertheless, a leader is not there just to organize tasks and direct people towards a common goal. They also represent a motivational figure, someone in charge to keep things on track even when the situation gets complicated (it does not have to be a "big deal", but everyone can have a bad day, and the leader has to know how to handle it); for these reasons, it is likely that an extra amount of work will have to be assigned to the head of the group.

5. Who is our leader, Madhumita Das?

Madhumita Das is a young Indian woman who has managed to reach success starting from the bottom and going all the way up to the top.

Madhumita was born in India in a city called Calcutta. From a very young age she was forced to take decisions which would shape her into becoming a passionate, curious and driven person. During her early years she didn't have a family: as a child, her father left home and soon after her mother fell ill. In her house, she was expelled by her grandparents, which forced her to search for a future on her own.

Indeed, fortune blessed her: she was welcomed by an NGO where she went to school and grew up. Madhumita was not always the star student; in fact, during her childhood, she was a rebellious girl. She was not influenced by society; instead, she preferred to think out of the box. Rather than settling for what her future was meant to be, she decided to shape her own future through her passions. This was a key point for her future success, as she manages to convey these passions through her work.

Later in her life, she was given the opportunity to travel to Madrid to do a Masters in corporate communication at IE University. After finishing her Masters she jumped into the work field, always with the aim of helping those in need. Madhumita's main objective is to encourage people to create a future for themselves. She believes that just studying is not enough; instead of this everyone should have a devotion in their lives and work to fulfil it. At the moment she is working as a business development executive for an online application called *Smartick*, an online application which teaches Maths to kids with the help of artificial intelligence.

6. "I am lucky and that is what keeps me going"

After hearing about her painful past and what she has managed to achieve we could only think about one more question: how could you keep on going even when you were all alone? Madhumita answered us by saying "I was not born in the best of circumstances, but I always believe that there are people who are worse-off and still they are surviving, so I am lucky and that is what keeps me going". After listening to her response we concluded that instead of complaining about her life, she makes sure to think positively and be grateful for the chances that life has granted her. This is the main reason why we chose her as our figure of a leader. We believe that a leader is not necessarily the noisiest person in the room, but rather the person who manages to make a change; someone who, in spite of everything, never surrenders. And Madhumita is a clear example of it.

7. How obstacles can be turned into opportunities:

If we were to define a "leader," probably the first thing that comes to our minds is related to all those figures in history who had, at some point in time, the ability or skill to lead people and nations to great results. Churchill or Obama for example as two of the most powerful politicians of their times; Mother Theresa and Mahatma Gandhi to mention a few more examples...but what do they all have in common? Haven't they changed the lives of millions of people? Haven't they supported or follow a specific mind-set until the very end? Haven't they made sacrifices for their cause?

Yet, the question is *"are leaders born with the ability to transform people's lives? Or do specific circumstances shape them?"* We guess it could be mixture of both. Although it is true that a seed of strong personality helps as a starting point, that does not mean that surpassing difficult obstacles has no impact on behaviour. Let's take Madhumita as an example, a young girl with a complicated background who has changed the life of many children by founding a series of NGOs. Her specific circumstances had so much impact on her as a person that she decided to transform people's lives for good. A special power, ability or capacity that she acquired by undergoing the same experience as those children under her protection. So yes, it does not take much to be good leader, with a great cause; just a strong conviction of driving people towards a better and constructive life.

The world has always been unpredictable, surprising us every single day of our lives, creating situations where we cannot anticipate or get over them. We have been taught to achieve our objective quickly with as few deviations and obstacles as possible. However, those who are successful in starting companies, or helping the most needed, decide to follow their expected path. They not only work with the surprises in such adventure, but also take advantage of it. For them, problems are a potential resource, not a disadvantage.

There are no such things as problems, just opportunities, if we view these problems as challenges. The key is to focus ourselves in setting our goals, and not on the plan that we initially drew up to get there. Being mature enough to think that your objective does not change, but accepting that how you would get there might change.

Madhumita is an example of this big idea where she has develop the ability to turn the unexpected into the profitable, leaving aside her difficult background and given a change and chance to her attitude towards situations. She has gone through a very transformative moment, where she has moved from an explorer to a leader.

8. Different leaders worldwide and comparison with Madhumita

If we think of great world leaders, we can all see great figures such as Barack Obama, Angela Merkel, Steve Jobs and many more. There are many different types of leaders in the world: we can find those who are focused on helping people, to supporting them, to getting the best out of each one, to leaders focused on giving orders, supervision of tasks, focused on the fulfilment of work.

A good example of a leader who supports and manages people would be Zinedine Zidane, the Real Madrid football coach who focuses on controlling the emotions of his players, ego control, motivation, etc. On the other hand, there are the leaders who we believe are focused on the completion of tasks, the distribution of work, the direction ... we would take Vladimir Putin as someone we feel is a leader focused on work, directing people and dictating orders. As you can see, we have put two very extreme cases, one very focused on people and the other very focused on the task.

And how does Madhumita fit in here? We believe that Madhumita fits into the profile of a leader focused on managing people as most of her work is focused on helping disadvantaged people. She is working as a business executive for Smartick, and for that reason she is in the situation of directing people and making decisions. That is why her profile as a leader would be a mix of both, focused mainly on people, but with some directive and decision making behaviour.

To conclude we must clarify that all types of leadership are good; each of them has strengths and weaknesses in different fields. Each type of leadership fits into some situation, so it is just a matter of *how to adapt* to them. Sometimes we must focus on strengthening people, controlling their emotions and getting the best out of them and other times we must focus on making complicated decisions, take the hard parts of work and organize people.

9. Applying leadership to ourselves: getting our group to work

We have seen throughout the chapter what a part of leadership is. But how did we apply it to our group project?

We had a problem: we did not know each other at the beginning of this journey.

The first day of class we were randomly assigned to a group. Most of our classmates had had a previous relationship with their teammates; however, in our case we were just complete unknowns forced to work together for a final presentation that we did not even understand. Probably not the desired situation in which we wanted to be. Yet it was the situation in which we were in, so we could either be frustrated for the rest of the course, or we could either accept it, get to know each other and make the best project we could. Fortunately, the latter was chosen.

The first thing we needed to do was to break the ice. At the end, we realized that we were pretty similar: we all studied the same degree, we had similar interests and worries regarding the university life, we were all very interested in social issues... So, what started as complete unknowns had evolved in just some minutes to a more inclusive workgroup.

10. The Importance of Trust

Of course, we knew that this was just the beginning. If we wanted to make a great project, we knew that we would have to be a great team. And, to make it possible, we needed to trust each other. Trust is, in the end, the key of success. The question was how to build it from scratch.

First of all, we had to give each other the benefit of the doubt. In other words, we had to assume that we all wanted to work, and that we would do it in the most professional manner. At the beginning, there were no "free-riders", and we all wanted to make the best project possible. Secondly, we had to leave our egos to one side. We had to be able to give in when necessary, and accept other people's ideas so as to advance and make a project *collectively*. Only then would we be able to claim that the project was "ours". Thirdly, we had to delegate. The tasks were divided between the different team members, and none of us would "steal" one which was not his or hers. We could help each other, of course, but only if we were first asked to do so. And finally, we needed time. In the end, it was only after several days and weeks working together that we certainly showed that we trust each other.

We are proud to say that we were able to make it. We were able to imagine and visualize the project, select a leader, define our tasks and goals, set and respect the time deadlines. And we made it together.

Maybe the most representative example of this trust is the interview with the leader: this was probably the most important part of the project, as thanks to it we would make the final video with parts of this interview. After spending weeks organising it, it ended up that only some of us could take part in the interview. However, by then, those who could not make it trusted those who could not to do the job well, and those who made it knew that they could trust others to take part in the post-interview work.

The main take-away: we started as complete unknowns and, after many weeks of work, we became a very cohesive team. And we also did a great project. The key to our success: trust, trust and trust.

11

Goal Setting

True leadership lies in guiding others to success. In ensuring that everyone is performing at their best, doing the work they are pledged to do and doing it well.

Bill Owens

We have seen in an earlier chapter how a leader can listen and communicate with a follower on the basis of their personal motivation, abilities and the overall objectives of the organisation.

One of the aims of Servant Leadership is to help the follower grow, which brings us to the first model we are going to look at here – GROW.[26]

GROW

This acronym stands for Goals, Reality, Options (and/or obstacles) and Way forward (or Will). While it was developed

---

[26] John Whitmore was one of the people primarily responsible for developing this coaching tool. You can see it in more detail in his book 'Coaching for Performance.'

for coaching it can also be applied for a specific relationship between a leader and a follower.

The leader's role in the first stage is to help the follower define their own 'dream goal' or ideal future situation. The next step is to clarify that goal so that it becomes a clear target that the follower can aim at. Finally the follower will have to established specific milestone and process goals along the way to the "Dream Goal" so that the follower has a clear path that they have to take.

Reality refers to the followers' current situation, what their present feelings are, the resources that they have available and the barriers that they are currently facing. The leader helps the follower discover why and what they need to change and what they are already doing to achieve their goals.

Options and obstacles looks at the path that the follower has to take to get their Dream Goal. It is about discovering how to get from their current reality to the desired state, brainstorming different directions, possibilities and figuring out ways past the different obstacles on the path.

The final element Way Forward or Will, is about choosing the right option of the ones discussed, setting a time plan for getting started on the goal and ensuring that the follower knows what success looks like and celebrates success when they achieve it.

Not only is it possible for a Leader to use the GROW model on others, but also on themselves.

SMART

When putting these GOALs into practice another useful tool is the SMART system. Depending on the guru you speak to the acronym has slight variations but we will take one of the variations that is widely accepted.

S stands for specific. When designing goals for individuals and teams it is necessary for them to be Specific. Recently I agreed with my students that I needed to lose weight. I did not simply say 'I need to lose weight', I specifically said '15 kilos.'

M is for measureable. It should be possible to measure the goals so you know if you are achieving them or not, and how close or far you are towards meeting them. In my own personal example it is very easy to measure weight loss with a weighing scales. It is also possibly to measure food intake and calorie intake on a daily basis. There are also many smart watches which give you an idea of how much energy you are also burning of with specific exercises and activities. In a business environment it could be number of sales made, time spent on projects, market share etc.

A is for achievable. Is this actually something that can be achieved? This stops it simply being a fantasy and means that even though the goal is 'stretching' it is possible, with effort, to achieve. 15 kilos sounds like a lot but I have done it before and I am not trying to do it in an unrealistic time frame (I have lost 12 kilos in four months.) As a leader it is very important to bear this in mind. Some leaders set unrealistic targets for their followers because they believe that it will motivate them further. The opposite is true. People give up early or without even trying when they realise it is unattainable. This links directly with Daniel Pink's theory as covered in the chapter on Motivation where he talks about Mastery of a task being tough, but not impossible.

R is for relevant. Again this has been mentioned in several places already. It is the leader's job to ensure that the goals and the vision they are communicating is clearly relevant to the followers. If they cannot see why it is important to them and why they should care then they will not put their heart into achieving the goal. In my case losing weight is relevant because it is related to my health. It is also relevant because it shows my students how to implement the SMART model. If I cannot do that then I should not teach them the model.

The final letter T stands for Time-bound. It is important to have a clear timeline for when you want to achieve the goal. This goes hand-in-hand with being specific and achievable. This is also something agreed with the follower. You can break the goal down into smaller parts that have to be achieved by certain dates or in certain timeframes. This will also help to create a certain sense of urgency and overcome procrastination.[27] In my case I agreed the goal of 4 months with my students to lose 15 kilos. I then used this timeline to keep me on track, know that I was running behind at different

---

[27] In the area of how deadlines help to overcome unproductive procrastination I suggest you watch the TED talk by Tim Urban on the procrastination monkey inside us all

stages and to encourage me to stick with the goal, for just another few weeks.

Key Takeaways

1. Listen first, speak second[28]
2. Acknowledging that someone has a point does not mean you are agreeing with them.[29]
3. When you have established an atmosphere of trust you can openly discuss goals and how to achieve them.
4. Goals are not only organizational but personal and it is important to align them.
5. "A spoonful of honey gets more results than a litre of vinegar".

---

[28] This is also reflected in the Steven Covey's work – 'seek first to understand and then to be understoood'.
[29] Getting Past No by William Ury develops this idea further.

12

Elsa Noguera

Dream Big

Jaime Herrera

Paula Munarriz

Part I: Our Leader

Insofar as defining what a leader is, or what leadership skills consist of, there can be no exact definition. We are all different, every context and situation is different, and we all have different perspectives. Throughout the time we spent on this project, we have learned that a leader is someone who understands that there is no right or wrong way to lead in different situations, someone who is able to motivate, inspire, create networks, and build respect.

Our chosen leader is Elsa Noguera. Elsa is a Colombian woman, born in Barranquilla, who became a prominent politician and an example for many. She is currently a politician and carries out work for her political party, but currently does not hold office. She was mayor of Barranquilla from 2012 to 2015, and then was summoned to become Minister of housing, city and territory. It's important to highlight everything that Elsa has accomplished throughout her life despite the challenges she has faced due to her physical disability. It's no secret that Elsa has struggled throughout her life with an illness that is known as over-calcification of the bones. This means that her bones are very fragile and easy to break. In fact, she has had to go through surgery multiple times and constantly uses crutches and canes when she walks. Still, this hasn't been an obstacle for Elsa but rather a challenge she tries to defeat in her everyday life.

The following is the draft of the interview we carried out with Elsa Noguera. We decided to ask her around 6 questions where she was able to share a little about different aspects of her life as well as her opinion regarding specific topics.

1. Who is Elsa Noguera?

Hello everybody, my name is Elsa Noguera. I am a cheerful and optimistic woman who is convinced that limits do not exist. We only create them in our minds. I love numbers, that's why I'm an economist, a specialist in finance with an MBA. I started my working life in the financial sector, in the field of research, until 10 years ago when I had the opportunity to enter the public sector, and my life changed forever.

2. What is your main motivation in life?

My main motivation is to serve and participate in the construction of a country with greater social justice. That is why I understood politics as that tool that allows us to participate in the decision making processes for the benefit of the part of the population that is most in need.

3. What is being a leader?

A leader is the person capable of inspiring others so that they can fulfill a collective purpose and that is precisely what we did in Barranquilla; Inspire the *Barranquilleros*, convince them that it was possible to live in a better city. I confess that it was not easy in 2008 when Alejandro Char invited me to be his finance secretary. At that time Barranquilla was totally broke, we owed money to everyone, there were no resources from which to make investments. But we implemented a management model with leadership and today we are the number one city in Colombia.

4. Are you born a leader or do you learn to be a leader?

We are not always born leaders, but on the way, we can learn to be leaders. That was my case, I never imagined I was going to be the mayor of Barranquilla, believe me, but I dared. I was not afraid of failure, and I was the first woman mayor elected by popular vote. And today what I like the most is that the girls in my city do not only dream of being carnival queens but they also want to be mayors.

5. What qualities must a leader possess and what do you consider to be the most important?

There are many traits that a leader must have. First, a leader must be a visionary with the capacity to dream big. To all of you, I say that if you still don't have dreams to conquer, look for them because a life without illusions, without goals to reach, is a sad life. Secondly, I believe the most important quality and the main thing that every leader should have is the ability to inspire moral authority. That is to say that a leader has to be consistent, they have to act according to what they say, they have to set a good example, in such a way that the people who follow you, the people who work with you do it because they love you, because you are admired and respected and not only for the authority that a position may confer. Remember that jobs and opportunities come and go, but the most beautiful thing in life is to conquer hearts, that remains forever.

6. Have the health problems you have had been an obstacle in your life?

As many of you know, I have used crutches much of my life to walk. Today, thank God I am much better and I only use a cane. However, this fragility that I had as a child in my bones has never been an obstacle for me. It has always been a challenge, a challenge to overcome. I want to give you a recent example; Two years ago, the president called me and invited me to accompany him in the housing ministry. I confess that I felt fear, it was something completely different. I was going to have to travel all over Colombia, to take helicopters, chalupas, to travel the territory a lot. But I never felt that I could not do it. Despite these fears, I dared, because that is what characterizes a leader. Everybody fears something at some point of their lives; this is what the uncertainty to the unknown produces. But what sets a leader apart is that we face our fears despite feeling them. I invite you all to dream big and you should know that you are capable of conquering the world if your hearts want to. I invite you to discover that great leader that we all have inside of us.

Part II: The Project

The initial project we had to put together was a video campaign on our chosen leader. At that point, we were a group of four university students, who were grouped not by choice, but by the selection of our professor. His goal was to group us with people we did not know before. At first, we did not understand why we were unable to pick our groups since we knew we would have to be able to work on a group project. Free riders are everywhere, and certainly, no one wants to have one of them in their group.

Our group members were Paula (Colombia), Jaime (Colombia), Mahaut (France) and Tomas (Argentina). From working together, we learned multiple things about ourselves, and with time, we became friends. Through participating in activities that seemed peripheral to the main project we built trust and understood the people we were, not just the roles we assigned each other.

Furthermore, we were assigned to develop a project around someone whom we consider to be a leader. By working together, and brainstorming on who we could choose to make our project about, we started to think big first. We all suggested wild ideas like soccer players, entrepreneurs, politicians, singers and more. But then, we realized that we needed to choose someone whom we could contact and speak to – a real person, a real leader. Then, Paula suggested that we could contact one of her family's acquaintances, Elsa Noguera. She explained who Elsa was, what she had accomplished and as a group, we agreed immediately and loved the idea. We had a Vision to bring our team together and give us focus. And that was just the start.

If we go over all the concepts that we tried to apply in the structure of our project, we would be extending this chapter way too much. Therefore, when determining which theory helped us the most throughout the development of our project we would say that the SMART (Specific, measurable, achievable, relevant, time-bound) goals were the one. Thanks to this concept we were able to determine the specific objectives needed to reach our vision.

Specific - All of the group members were aware that we were going to be participating in a creative project along with a bunch of strangers for the following 5 months. Although it wasn't clear at first, we brainstormed what was exactly needed to be done in order to determine the real purpose of this project.

Measurable - It was important for us to measure the length of this project in order to determine what were the requirements. After the weeks passed by, we realized that the concepts presented in class were provided as tools for us to use when completing the project. These tools were also useful for building the proper bases to handle effective communication and relationships.

Achievable - As was already mentioned, we found ourselves somewhat confused at the starting point of the project. But we then realized that it was going to take a lot of creativity and effort in order to develop the best project possible. We needed to find a way to relate the leadership concepts with the project itself. This would be achievable by using the proper tools and guidance.

Relevant - We believed that with great effort valuable lessons would come along to cherish in the future. Learning how to work with others and building leadership skills were some of the benefits that this project left us with.

Time-Bound - We believed that we were able to finish this project within the time-length of the semester. We just had to be in constant awareness of the important concepts that we could apply to the project. In turn, we also used them in personal situations as it was already mentioned. Since we were building up this innovative project, we didn't have a clear structure of the different stages of the project. With the help of the teacher, we found spaces where we could share our thoughts and opinions about the features of the project in general. With this mechanism we had a chance to review the aspects of the project on a regular basis.

In addition, when we decided to contact Elsa, we needed to set SMART goals about the interview itself. We had to define the specific questions we wanted to ask her. That meant deciding what we wanted to learn. We had to decide when we could interview, how long we would need before the video was created, translated, edited, how to make the video relevant to us, and was this all achievable in the time we were setting ourselves. We planned all of this using the relevant elements of the SMART goals system and then put it into practice.

As we get to the end of this project, we can say that we're impressed by how this idea turned out to be more developed than expected, leaving several thoughts and lessons to bear in mind.

- This was all possible thanks to the motivation we had throughout the evolution of the project. We believe it's important to mention this since it was relevant for us to keep that motivation is something we all believe and which we were capable of making great. We kept ourselves motivated by building strong interpersonal relationships and keeping our goal in mind at all time.
- Having this in mind, we went step by step trying to give it our best. As the weeks went by we realized that the course was providing us with a wide-range of theories on what this is all about: leadership. So it was from this point on that we started to evaluate how to apply leadership to the project itself and real-life situations. We decided that leadership is not

just something you study, it is something you live.

- The fact that at the beginning most of us considered each other to be strangers also motivated us to build and maintain relationships with people from different backgrounds and with distinct attributes. We started to understand the way of being of each other in order to handle effective communication. And when some of us lost track, we were always there for each other to guide and help in the way we could. We learned about the need for clear communication and trust and how they help a team grow.
- From interviewing Elsa, we not only felt what she went through, but it helped us realize that sometimes the obstacles we feel we have are self-imposed shackles.
- We also learned that there are many people all around the world that have gone through unthinkable situations and that everyone has a story to tell.

If we go back one year most of us can say that we never imagined ourselves participating in a project like this one. We thought it was more probable that we would participate in an entrepreneurship fair rather than in the publishing of a book.

But that is part of what leadership is about, as Elsa says, "dream big and you should know that you are capable of conquering the world if your hearts want to."

13

Persuasion

The key to successful leadership today is influence, not authority.

Ken Blanchard

If you think of persuasion as manipulating others for your own selfish purposes, then this is not the chapter you are hoping for.

Persuasion as we define it here, is the ability to get people to do things without violence. Some people believe that this must be negative because if it was good for them then they would already be doing it. This is less the case than you might think. Persuading someone to eat healthily, to work well with others, to stop smoking etc. are all positive for the individual who you are trying to persuade.

In the context of Leadership, some of the ways that an understanding of Persuasion helps you are the following:

- Communicate your Vision effectively

- Motivate people to put the vision into practice
- Ensure that they feel accountable for their actions
- Change negative behaviours and processes
- Implant positive change in the lives of your followers and organisation
- Build trust
- Establish your credibility among them.

Going back to some of the ideas in the classic 'How to Win Friends and Influence People' by Dale Carnegie, written in the 1930s, it becomes very clear, very quickly that persuasion need not be a negative thing. Carnegie makes recommendation such as 'develop a genuine interest in the other person', 'be sympathetic with the other person's desires', and 'dramatize your ideas.'

James Borg says that Persuasion can be expressed in the formula:

Empathy + Sincerity = Persuasion

As you can see from these initial ideas, the first element of Persuasion is to think in terms of the other person's interests. This goes back to earlier chapters in this book which talk about understanding other people's personalities and what makes them tick, and creating a vision that is relevant for them.

The 5 Cs

One of the easiest ways to persuade people is through the art of telling stories. Statistics are fantastic for supporting arguments and for justifying a course of action. Stories are what move people. You might feel that you are not a storyteller or that you would have to spend a lot of time, imagination and effort creating a good story but this is not true. We will look at the 5Cs formula in a moment.

Stories are useful because they:

- Are easy to understand
- Are easy to remember
- Make sense of complicated ideas.
- Give concrete examples of abstract concepts.
- Click with a brain that has evolved over thousands of years listening to stories.
- Bring emotion to sterile facts.
- Give a roadmap for how to act.

To create a motivation story, or even a story to sell an idea you need five elements:

Character. This could be as simple as 'My friend Bob...' It could even be an organisation or company but it works better with someone you can imagine in your mind's eye.

Conflict. The problem that your character has. Why he is not satisfied. What is going wrong, or has just gone wrong for him.

Cure. The solution to the problem.

Change. How Bob has changed as a result of the 'Cure.'

Carry out message. What is the key idea that you want people to remember from your story?

Over the years I have had many students who believe that they are not creative, and could never tell a decent story. After I have explained this very simple formula I have seen thousands of people create incredible stories in as little as fifteen minutes. A week later, people who heard the stories can still remember them. As a result I see people regularly using this formula successfully in presentations afterwards. I suggest you try it and see how it helps you persuade people more effectively and ensure that they remember your message. And there, in one paragraph, is the 5Cs in action.

Aristotle

While it seems a strange on a book about Leadership in the 21st Century to go back an ancient Greek source, I have found that by understanding the three key elements of artistic persuasion as laid out by Aristotle, it gives you a straightforward structure for thinking about your own efforts to persuade, ethically, your followers to take a certain course of action.

The three main elements of persuasion according to Aristotle are:

- Ethos
- Pathos
- Logos

Ethos refers primarily to the credibility we have with the people we are trying to persuade. Do they treat us with respect, do they believe us, do they trust us, and do they think we are an authority on the subject. Some people have this Ethos purely because of their official position in an organisation. A true leader however makes sure they have it through their own character. In order to have Ethos with your followers they have to believe that you are trying to persuade them out of selfless reasons, that you are consistent in your behaviour, that they can trust you to follow through on what you are promising and, of course, that they believe what you are saying.

Pathos refers to the emotional arguments that you use when trying to persuade. People believe that they are more logical than they actually when it comes to taking decisions. The reality is that we often make spur of the moment decisions based on how we are feeling, how we feel about the person speaking to us, and what our first emotional response is to something. We then use our powerful brains to justify the decision we have just taken.[30] Therefore it is very important when thinking about how to persuade your followers to take into account their emotions – not to manipulate them, but rather to understand how they will impact on their decision to follow your vision or not.

---

[30] "How We decide" by Jonah Lehrer goes into this topic in detail. It is a fascinating journey into the mind and decision making process of the average process. Not only will it help you understand why others take the decisions they do, but it will also give you a better insight into the way you make up your mind.

The last element Aristotle covers is Logos, which refers to the rational arguments you use to persuade people. You may move people initially with Pathos but very often you will need strong, rational arguments for them to repeat to themselves afterwards so they can explain to themselves why they continue to follow your vision and direction.

Together these three elements will remind you to craft your message to your followers deliberately and consciously and not simply by using a collection of off-the-cuff comments.

Take Away Messages

1. Persuasion does not have to be manipulation.
2. Ethical persuasion comes from a place of empathy, sincerity and a genuine interest in the other person.
3. People are hardwired to listen and remember stories.
4. You can construct a story quickly and effectively with the 5Cs formula.
5. Classical persuasion consists of a combination of personal credibility, appeals to emotion and rational arguments.

14

Davide Dattoli

Shaping a new way of working

Empathy + sincerity = persuasion

Dea Suliashvili

Guglielmo Sirolli

Cristiano Scrocchia

Yannick Scheurer

Davide Dattoli is a young Italian entrepreneur with the dream of connecting together all the innovative tech industries to promote growth and innovation locally and globally. He started this project before achieving a university degree and he is now the CEO and co-founder of Talent Garden (Tag): a company with the purpose of reaching out to the tech talents in Europe to give them the possibility of creating a huge network of talents and innovators.

The company operates with a fairly simple business plan: rent a large space where you can fit many desks and then rent them to small tech start-ups who will develop and grow before moving out. However, Davide and his team have created much more than a simple co-working space; by investing strongly in events, social platforms and community managers, as he will later explain in the interview, Talent Garden managed to create a community where people interact between each other to achieve progress with their business and sometimes to merge together to create a new company. This community has been growing and spreading non-stop since its inauguration in 2012 with the opening of the first campus in Brescia, Italy.

The beauty of the company is how it is generating a community which is not limited by the campus boundaries, in fact, it reaches out to all the other campuses around Europe and probably someday to campuses outside Europe. Davide strongly believes in the power of technology and community to the point where he is also trying to revolutionize education; a few campuses have dedicated some space to what is now known as the Tag Innovation School, the idea is to give brief but intense courses that can be of many types: from growth-hacking to business data analysis as well as digital marketing, coding and many others. These courses last less than a year and are aimed at giving the student the tools to work for three to five year jobs, this is how the world is spinning nowadays, people like to change jobs after some time and the old system of studying three years plus a Masters to work for the same job for a lifetime only applies to students of medicine. We had the opportunity to interview him through skype and collected information to detect his personality and what makes him the great leader he is today.

1. **How was Talent Garden born and what is the main goal of this company?**

→ As Talent Garden, we started in 2012 and we are now in more than 24 different cities and 8 countries with a model which is trying to bring power to the local tech innovators of the main European cities. We started with a co-working business and later introduced as well an education and event side to the company. Everything started with the idea that Europe is totally fragmented and there is a need get the tech talents to connect to each other and to boost innovation around Europe. Talent Garden decided to fulfill this need and act as a platform to help locally and globally the different tech talents as well as start-ups, freelancers and other talents in the Tech industry to connect and grow together.

2. **What are the core values of Talent Garden and how do you make sure a new employee meets these values as soon as possible?**

→ For us defining the culture of Talent Garden is a way to define our operating system, how people have to make decisions, how people have to interact with each other. It is very clear for us and we usually make presentations to employees about what it means to work in Talent Garden and career growth and opportunities, so that when you enter you immediately know where you are and what different levels you can achieve here. There are no possibilities of uncertainty, miscommunication or unfairness. Everything is very clear, everything is transparent. You know where you are, you know what the different levels in TAG are, and what is required to reach the next level.

3. **How do you make sure that everyone in the Tag family is involved and collaborates in the community?**

→ We have three ways to facilitate the arrival and the future permanence of a new member: Firstly, we have some community team members, these are people who are in charge of creating and connecting the community between the different networks and students that are in the campuses. The second one is a tech platform that collects all of the Taggers online where you can find the various passions and various skills of every talent in the community and try automatically to bring connection, you can search for a particular skill on the platform and then write a message or invite for a coffee with the Tagger that seems to be satisfying your needs.

Lastly, we manage to connect Taggers thanks to a series of events that we organize during the years; the events are not directed to all the whole Talent Garden community but instead are organized in a way to bring together people with similar needs and interests.

4. **Regarding yourself as a leader: what are your main strengths and weaknesses and is there anything you would like to change about your personality?**

➔   I will start from the bad side: I may have some problems with managing people, it is easier for me to get along with someone that shares my same interests and behaviours. However, one of the main core values of Talent Garden is entrepreneurship which means that by joining Talent Garden you are expected to bring your own project and there is no one to tell you what to do.

I do not want as a leader to be someone who controls other people, I do not feel like I am smarter than other people around me and this is why I like to leave free choice to my colleagues and Taggers inside the community.

This brings me to my strength which in my opinion is the way, with the help of the team, we manage to empower the people to develop their own activities and projects inside Talent Garden.

5. **Building on to this, have you ever been through a hard conversation, maybe having to fire someone from their job or finding yourself in an uncomfortable situation due to the behaviour of a Tagger inside the campus?**

→ Absolutely, regarding firing employees I always say that the is never a individual problem with the single person but instead it is about the need of the company, it may happen that you hire someone that at that time in that moment was the real need of the company. However, as the company grows and the ecosystem around this position has changed so much that the profile that the employee is working on is no longer the right one.

Another core value of Talent Garden is trust and transparency, what I normally say is that losing a job is completely normal, it can happen to anyone - myself included. It is part of the growth of a company and the growth of the individual's profile. It is better to share the problem instead of ignoring it and pretending everything is working perfectly.

6. **Regarding your relationship with employees; are you open to advice and how much independence do you give your employees?**

→ From my point of view, I am very open with my employees. I do not have an office. I only use a desk which by the way is available for the use of whoever needs it. I firmly believe that there should be no wall or protection between the leader and his colleagues: everyone is on the same level. We are trying to create a project, we are trying to create a company, the importance is the results, not the level between employees, this is the reason we try to keep the organizational structure as flat as possible: we don't need people that do what they are told, we need people that do what the data tells them to do.

7. **Can you name a person that empowered you as a leader and how did they impact your life?**

→ Based on my experience there was not one person and one moment when that happened, but almost everyone and each period from the past I can say are important experiences that shaped my identity as a leader. I personally learn from different types of people and most of the time they are coming from the person I would not think of and they play less importance in my daily life, though in reality, they bring many transformations in my business approach.

For example, the person I received a big lesson from which I did not expect to happen was when I was an employee of another company. Honestly, at least for me, my boss was not a good boss and he showed me what kind of a leader I did not want to be in future. You could not enter his working space when he was inside and you could not meet him. It seems incredible but unfortunately, it happens very frequently and I think that this hierarchical process and the big distinction between the boss and the employees is very stupid and does not make sense, because both have the same interest for the company and these artificial barriers are useless.

8. **What are the failures that made the greatest impact on you and the mistakes that helped you to become the leader you are today?**

→ All the times that someone said no without any reason. Because it is the time when you think most about everything when you really try to work on yourself and try to understand how to get better, because it seems incomprehensible to you why that happened. Personally, for me all the time when someone said no without giving any explanation had really good consequences since that was the time when I tried to improve much more.

9. **Do you think that the leader is born or made? Does it take practice and time to learn leadership skills or is it something you are naturally born with?**

→ I think leadership skills are for a period of time on a specific project. You don't grow as a leader and it is not something natural, it is something that you have to learn and understand how to be a good leader. I think that since now I know the activities and projects of the company very well, I can lead it for next three to five years successfully, but maybe in ten years from now the person currently working for me can lead the company better and there is nothing bad about it.

10. **What are the challenges that the leaders face today?**

→ I would say recruiting talent. It can be easy to convince the person to work for the company, but it is very difficult to keep them for many years. The world is moving so fast nowadays and we face so many changes, people also want to keep up with those changes and search for new jobs every two to three years. From the perspective of the company, which invests and puts a huge effort in the development of every employee in the first year, it is a big loss that they leave the company in the second year. So again, the biggest challenge for leaders of today is to keep those talents for a longer period and allow that to create something bigger and valuable and not only small short-term goals.

11. What would you advise the young leaders to avoid such kind of a problem?

→ To empower and involve people. Not only make them work for the company but make them feel that they are important and in fact, they are the company themselves. It is a question of communication and empowerment.

12. What are the challenges Talent Garden faces today and how do you see the expansion of your company in the future?

→ It is again about leadership and about people. It is important is to understand how to involve the best people in the different cities and empower them so that they can replicate what you already created in the other cities of Talent Garden. And honestly, it is very difficult because before you had to involve 5-10 people every year and next year we are going to be around 100 people. How can you really find the best talent and how can you give them the possibility to make every idea happen?

13. What is the one thing every young entrepreneur who is aiming to become a leader in future should learn?

→ It may sound pretty obvious; do not believe in your idea but in the people that you are able to attract because a company and a project is not about the idea itself but it's about the quality of the people that are working on that project because at the end it is only way to create something big, sustainable and that works. So the advice here is to really focus on trying to attract the best people who have the qualities for the project you want to build.

14. To conclude, what makes you most proud of Talent Garden and maybe share some advice to future leaders?

→ Yes, sure. Again, the most important thing is the quality of the people you involve in your organization and I am very proud of every member of Talent Garden.
The advice is very similar to what I said before, understand your role and mission, why you have to work for the company you are leading, how you can find new talents and how to bring the best ones into your team.

*

Davide Dattoli and his inspiring professional journey can be an example for every potential leader that hard work always pays off. Since a young age, Davide was very determined and committed to his wishes and goals. He was never afraid of having big dreams and plans.

One lesson you should definitely learn from Davide Dattoli is that the success of a team is not only the accomplishment of a leader, but achievements are shared between each individual member. He highlighted the importance of involving the most talented and hard-working people in your team and always putting a lot of effort into making them feel that they are valued and respected in the company.

Davide is very open to new ideas and advice. He respects his co-workers and always tries to communicate with them, listen to their suggestions and involve each person in organizational matters. He believes that the key to success is empowering each person in his team, give them the opportunity to grow and make them feel that they play an important role in success and development of the company. Thanks to this transparent and friendly environment in his organization, he created a strong team spirit and made everyone dedicated to the same mission and goal. He suggests that every young entrepreneur and leader should understand clearly what their role is in the organization. Davide believes that leadership is not something you are born with, but the skill that always comes with knowledge and experience. Leaders should always try to improve and grow further. He never stops working on himself and that is why even in such a rapidly changing business world, TAG successfully continues its expansion every day.

15

Emotional Intelligence

Everyone who's ever taken a shower has an idea. It's the person who gets out of the shower, dries off and does something about it who makes a difference.

Nolan Bushnell

One of my favourite books at present is called the Chimp Paradox[31].   It breaks down our brain and uses easy to understand metaphors to explain how we think, how we sabotage ourselves, and how we interact with others. The two central 'characters' in the book are the Chimpanzee and the Human, reflecting the twin horses of emotion and reason.

The Chimpanzee reflects the emotional part of our brain, which is much stronger than our rational part – when it is awake. It reacts defensively, aggressively, sexually - but not rationally. Many things wake up the Chimpanzee and our biology has trained us throughout our evolution to listen to the adrenalin,

---

[31] This is a self-help, coaching, reader-friendly version of brain science, productivity enhancing book by Dr. Steven Peters who has helped, among others, many British Olympians achieve their dreams.

cortisol and other natural drugs that the chimpanzee releases into our body over the deep thinking human. Jumping out of the way of an oncoming car, or fighting off an attacker, can save our lives and can be excellent short term survival strategies. However, living a life controlled by our inner chimpanzee is generally a terrible long term strategy.

Emotional Intelligence

Up to the 1990s the intelligence that concerned most was people was IQ and centred largely on our ability to master numbers and words. Since the 1990s and especially after the book by the same name[32] Emotional Intelligence (EQ) is recognized as equally important. When I described EQ to my mother she thought I was simply talking about 'common sense' and because EQ is now used to refer to everything under the sun, it also has many detractors.

The reason EQ is included in a book on leadership is the importance that emotions have in the lives of every person – it is in fact why we need leaders and not just managers. There is a recognition in a world where robots and computers can increasingly do everything that humans can, and often better,

---

[32] Emotional Intelligence By Daniel Goleman is a classic. Despite the fact that it was published in 1995 and Goleman has written several books since, including ones on leadership, and there are many other books on the subject, I would strongly recommend that you start with this book and go from there. All the information in it is still relevant – the human brain changes much, much more slowly than technology.

that what sets us apart is precisely what people felt for so long that made us less humans – emotions.   And that if a leader, if they want to create a vision that inspires, a motivated group of followers, a team that works effectively together, and a climate where conflict is constructive and not destructive.

Goleman's work covers five main areas that we must be aware of as leaders:

1. Self-awareness
2. Self-management
3. Self-motivation
4. Social-awareness
5. Social-skill

Self-awareness: If we are not aware of our own emotions then we will be at their mercy. By understanding what our emotions are, how they affect us and how they affect others, we can become 'better pilots of our lives'.   This means that we have accurately assess and monitor our emotions.   This is the cornerstone skill before we deal with the others.

Self-management: Being aware of our emotions and emotional reactions is one thing, controlling them is another. Using the example of the previous section, the objective here is to cage (not kill) the chimpanzee. Understanding that if you do not deal effectively with anger, it can build up into uncontrollable rage, sadness to mild depression and worrying to anxiety.   And this is only the impact that uncontrolled negative emotions have on ourselves – there is also the impact that these extreme emotions can have on those who are following us that we must take into account.

When you realise that there is a problem you can start working on fixing it. Reframing is one technique that can be used, where you change the way you look at a problem and see it as a learning or growth opportunity (see the chapter on 'Doing the Hard Things'). Or you look at a situation from the perspective of the person who is making you angry.

Other techniques include physical exercise to work the negative natural drugs out of our body. Goleman talks about the amygdala hijack, where the stress hormones released into the body take time (hour and even days) to dissipate, but because of successive things that make you angry, there is no opportunity to work these stress hormones out of our body and they simply build on each other in successive waves until we are no longer in control and rage takes over. Physical exercise helps to use up that hormone and reduce the chance of an 'amygdala' hijack.

Create distance between you and other people in that moment so that your body has an opportunity to naturally cool down, you get the chimpanzee out of the driving seat and the human back in control.

The opposite of distance is where you become fully present in the moment, using mindfulness techniques, to examine who you are feeling, what is really happening, and counteracting the "narrowing' effects of anger through forced widening of your awareness to your surroundings. A word of warning – if you are close to the amygdala hijack, I suggest creating some distance first (even if that means forcing a smile, saying you will be back in a moment and going to the bathroom to take deep breaths.)

"If you speak when angry, you'll make the best speech you'll ever regret."

Groucho Marx

For an effective toolkit to take control of your own emotions "The Green Platform" by Declan Coyle[33]. We are not responsible for the stimuli that happen in our lives – the traffic jams, someone else getting the promotion we had been expecting, a flight being cancelled, a sick child, a failed exam. And most of the time we cannot control our initial emotional reaction. However after that initial reaction we have a choice – to go to the Red Platform, and only see the negative of the situation. On the Red Platform we can react, and get angry, and complain and focus on the unfairness of it all.

Or else we can go to the Green platform where we step back from the situation, decide that we are going to take control of

---

[33] Declan Coyle is a wonderful example of a leader himself. Overcoming extreme difficulty in his own personal life, he practices what he preaches when it comes to the advice he gives other as a life and business coach. Personally I love his writing style and how easy it is to relate to what he says and apply it in your everyday life. I have only read his book twice but when I finish writing this one I will be going back for a third time.

our feelings rather than be at their mercy. There we can decide that if it's something as small as waiting an extra 10 minutes in the queue for a coffee that at the end of the day it is not that important and we are not going to get angry about it. That we acknowledge the initial feeling do not blame ourselves for that initial feeling, but then be proactive about deciding to see it in another light, or take importance away from it, or be empathetic with the person who is causing the feelings in us.

To illustrate this I love the story I heard many years ago, and for the life of me I cannot remember where I heard it, of a woman who had suffered terribly in a relationship with a man. When asked if she still hated him and felt anger towards him she replied that she had let that go because she 'didn't want him living rent-free in her head.' By letting go, she was taking back control of her life and her emotions.

This last example is important because as a leader you will be provoked, depressed, stressed, frustrated and disappointed by others on a regular basis. You will also, most likely, create all of those reactions in some of your followers at one stage or another.

Self-motivation: In the face of difficult situations a leader has to be able to motivate themselves. As many people have said 'it is lonely at the top' and if you are looking for others to motivate you, instead of you motivating them, you may be waiting for a while. Before helping others you have to develop the ability to stay enthusiastic and positive despite feedbacks.

This means that you have to control your own impulses, develop an ability to enter the optimal state of concentration[34] known as "Flow", and see failure as an opportunity to learn and improve.

Social awareness refers basically to the concept of empathy. In the chapter on communication we looked at how to listen to and create rapport with another person, in the chapter on Persuasion we showed that empathy was an essential element. When it comes to being a leader, being able to take the perspective of your followers is key. For some people, rather than taking a course on leadership, they would be better served by a course on listening and empathy – that way you will be able to identify what motivates your followers, what potential obstacles will stop them achieving the goals of the team or the organisation, and also how they will perceive your vision.

Social skill is the ability to persuade and influence others, to manage their emotions, to adapt to others mood and to get them to adapt theirs. This is the skill that many people who want to be leaders desire. However, before developing this skill (covered in other chapters in this book) it is essential to become emotional self-aware and develop empathy first.

A leader has to look after themselves before leading others

---

[34] "Flow, the secret to happiness" by Mihaly Csikszentmihalyi gives you a much better idea of the objective state and how to achieve it.

One of the areas already mentioned here is 'self-regulation'. If a leader is going to lead, then they need to be able to control their own emotions. One of the things that some leaders make the mistake of believing is the quote by Thomas Edison 'The chief function of the body is to carry the brain around'. This errs principally because it treats the body and the brain as two separate entities as opposed to intimately linked, indivisible parts. The brain itself is just another organ in the body, influenced by and influencing the others.

A leader needs to take care of their own body if they are going to lead effectively. While it is normal that a person will go through periods of extreme stress and the leader will force themselves onto great lengths as both an example and a driving force for their followers, this should not be a long term strategy. If it is, then then body will betray you, and your ability to lead into the future will be impaired – either through mental exhaustion, an ability to find creative solutions, flaring up at others at the wrong moment, or an inability to lift one's own spirts and then inspire others.

I believe this section is important because many leaders have a tendency to push themselves harder than others. It is necessary to develop strategies to make sure that your body and brain work as allies, not master and slave. This means:

- Regular, good sleep.
- Healthy diet.
- Exercise.

- Work-life balance (what that is depends on each person and your personal circumstances, but a life dedicated 100% to work will deliver sub-par work)
- Mindfulness (as Declan Coyle points out, the brain is constantly making us live in the past and in the future but we can only truly be happy in the present).

The road is long and those of us who have been running on it for a while realise the importance of looking after oneself first before we can look after others properly. It reminds me of the (what always strikes me as chilling) instructions they give you when you are about to take off in an airplane. If you have children you should put on your own oxygen mask first and then theirs.

Key Takeaways

1. Emotional intelligence is a key element of being an effective leader
2. You have to make sure that your inner chimpanzee is not in control, and be aware of other's inner chimpanzee
3. Emotional self-awareness is the first step.
4. Learn how to control emotions so that they do not control you
5. Empathy before persuasion.
6. We cannot choose the stimuli in our lives, or even the first reaction to these stimuli but we can choose whether we go to Green or the Red platform.

7. We must look after ourselves first, especially our bodies, if we want to operate at peak efficiency. Only then can we lead others.

16

Iôna de Macêdo
No Pain, No Gain

Andres Saavedra
Michelle Salgado

This chapter will be divided in two areas; our campaign and our leader. Through this we want to firstly demonstrate how we have worked these past months secondly through our personal accounts why our leader has demonstrated characteristics and qualities that make her a great person to follow.

Part I: The Project

1. Entering the Unknown
On the first day of class we did not know each other and we came from many different programs. We were not even sure what awaited us on this course.   When it came to choosing a leader that we would interview for a video campaign we decided to choose Iôna de Macêdo as she really inspires us.

The task we set ourselves was to learn about leadership, meet each other, work together as a team, understand each other's culture, organize the professional filming of the interview and promote Iôna as an excellent example of leadership, all while trying to study for every other subject, meet our deadlines, and try to have a life. Seems simple, right? It wasn't at first, but we made it so.

2. Challenges Encountered

We encountered four main challenges during these past few months. These were:

1. Initial lack of trust: At the start of the project we didn't really know each other. Personally, we didn't really know anything about each other, we may have seen each other around university but that was the extent of it. This was challenging because we had to learn to trust each other and figure out each other's working styles and work together effectively.

2. Problems with schedules: Our group is divided between two degrees, two people are studying communication and two are studying business administration. However, even though two people are studying Business, they're not in the same class, making it hard for them to know each other beforehand as well as having the same schedules. Due to this, we all had different schedules which made it hard to meet, since rarely we all were free at

the same time. Also, Iôna was really busy this past semester so we had to arrange a time that was both suitable for both us and her. This was probably our biggest challenge.

3. Quality standards: Another challenge we faced, was to produce a work of high quality for Iôna. This was due to various situations such as time-management, final exams, spring break, amongst others. However, we have made sure that the project has turned out to be a success regardless of other external factors.

4. Efficiency when working: We have other courses and classes with final exams in April/May, however, we were successful in optimizing our time and work in order to have a finished video that we could present in class and to Iôna.

3. What we have learnt so far

This project has taught us a lot in such a short time, however I think that these six main points are worth mentioning:

1. Teamwork: We have learnt to come together and work around our schedules since we don't all study the same degree, and give our best to make sure this project turns out great.

2. Negotiation: We mainly learnt about negotiation when arranging meeting times and days.

3. Personalities and Different Cultures: We all have different personalities and we come from different

countries but we learnt to work around them and work really well together.

4. Laugh and Smile: We laughed and smiled a lot during filming and the project which is always a good thing since life can't always be too serious.

5. Motivation: We learnt from Iôna how motivation and hard work can lead you to success in life and to achieve both your goals and dreams.

6. Determination: Similarly we learnt through Iôna that never giving up and believing in your dreams can lead you to achieve them.

Part II: Our Leader

Iôna de Macêdo is one of the leaders who has more impact in our immediate context as IE University students. She is the Academic Director of the Bachelor of Communications and Digital Media at IE University and is one of the most representative figures of the department she heads at the University. Iôna is a person who has proven to be a leader throughout her life because when any problem appeared to her, she knew how to get ahead successfully, achieving her goals and helping others as well. She is an adaptive leader, as a result of her participation in different areas, working with people of different backgrounds, cultures and ways of thinking. She worked in companies of medium size to leading corporations in their area worldwide, occupying positions of great responsibility that required a lot of sacrifice.

There are many examples throughout her professional life that can be used to demonstrate her leadership skills, how a good leader should act, etc., but this time I will only talk about a personal characteristic and the idea that it generates in its environment. Throughout her life Iôna had to deal with several situations in where decisive and high-impact decisions had to be taken. All these experiences forged Iôna's personality, giving her the privilege of having a highly developed emotional intelligence. Emotional intelligence is, according to Goleman, "the ability to recognize your own feelings and emotions as well as those of others and then to use that information to manage those emotions and relations". Every word of that sentence comes alive when analyzing her life.

She had to face different challenges in her professional career, from being one of the few women to holding important positions in her sector and in countries where the culture is very different, to being a wife and a mother. She had to make many sacrifices throughout her life, sacrifices that not all people are willing to make or can bear, but she was always willing to take them with happiness and hope that through them she could help her family and society. She knew how to control her emotions and those of her environment in order to meet her objectives, but also so that each of the people who were involved could grow as a person.

"Before starting this project I did not know Iôna personally, I had only heard a little about her when some friends commented about their classes. When we decided to work with her to carry out this work, I began to investigate what was the community's concept of her and whether they considered her a leader or not. I spoke with several of her students and people who had the opportunity to work with her or attended one of her classes. I was very surprised to hear the concept she represented.

Iôna is considered within the society as an example to follow, because she is a person of great professional success but especially for her charisma. All the people said that she not only cares about the academic part but also about the human part, that she is a demanding person but she does it because she wants everyone to develop the best version of themselves, that is a person with values and principles that seeks to help others and is always willing to collaborate when someone needs help.

After listening to these comments and being able to meet her in person, I can say with all certainty that she is a great example to follow. She is the living concept of Excelsior, to give the best version of each one, in every activity that takes place and to be able to help others to do the same. There are few people who pass on that feeling to others, and Iôna manages to do it with every person she meets. Without the need to know her, just by listening to the impact she has caused in the lives of many, she makes you think about many aspects of your life. That makes her a great leader, she stops being just one person to follow and becomes a set of principles and ideas that others want to follow."

- Andres Saavedra

"As Andres mentioned, this was the first time he and another member of our group met Iôna. Unlike them, I already knew her, but I didn't know the extent of her story until we interviewed her. I met Iôna back in 2015 when I had just turned 18. It's going to sound very stereotypical but similarly to other 18 year olds, I wasn't really sure what I wanted to do with my life. I was doing a degree that I soon found out wasn't right for me, my parents were going to send me back to Mexico and ground me for life after they found out I was flunking all my classes with the exception of maybe one or two (and those weren't going that well either), I was partying every night, making bad decisions all the way. Basically, to summarize my life at that moment; it was a huge and total mess. I didn't want to be the cliché college dropout so I had to make a change, I needed to change my situation and improve it, not just focus on partying and thinking that the future was far away when in reality 4 years go by in the blink of an eye. I wanted to make the most of my experience and thankfully as fate would have it, Iôna was there to help. The January of 2015 was when Iôna was going to start her position as the new Director of the Bachelor of Communications and Digital Media Program. I don't know if she knows this but giving me the opportunity to change degrees changed positively a lot of aspects in my life and because of that I'm eternally grateful to her.

After we interviewed Iôna, I realized that I only knew a small piece of her story, I knew she worked in the media industry and that she spent time working in Latin America and Europe at Sony, but I didn't know about all the sacrifices she had to make and how she had to prove herself along the way. After listening to her answering our questions, I realized that there is more to her than meets the eye. I knew her teaching style after I had the opportunity of having her as a teacher in 2017, but after hearing her interview, I realized that the characteristics she currently possesses she has had them through all her professional life. She is an extremely determined person that pushed herself through her young adult life in order to get to where she is now, even though there were many obstacles and sacrifices to be made along the way. If you meet her now, you can clearly see that she is also an extremely charismatic and supporting person. She cares deeply about her students and is constantly involved with them and their projects. It is not hard to believe that she was the same way before she joined the senior management staff at IE. Another characteristics that she possesses are that she is very passionate about her work and she is very knowledgeable about the media industry, I'm always in awe when she talks about her contacts and the people she has met during her work-life.

Iôna inspires me to be a leader because she not only represents a successful career woman, but she represents that dreams and goals do come true through hard-work, dedication and motivation. She is especially inspiring to many young women because gender equality in the work-place is an issue that is constantly challenged due to the inequality in pay between men and women. Additionally, due to all the recent sexual assault scandals in Hollywood, it is evident that being a woman in the media industry is certainly not easy. Finally, sacrificing a lot of aspects of your family-life and missing important events in order to focus on your professional career is not easy. Keeping the balance between family-life and work-life is not easy, and I can imagine it's especially hard when you're a woman. I don't have any children but I can imagine the need to be with them all the time and the immense sacrifice of not being able to. Because of all these reasons I admire her greatly and I sincerely believe that she is a great person to follow, and I'm sure that many people would agree with me.

We're really grateful to Iôna for agreeing to do the interview. We want to thank her for allowing us to get to know her and giving us an insight into her professional life. We all think that she not only is a great leader but she is also extraordinary as a person. She is definitely someone people should look up to."

-Michelle Salgado

17

Trust

"The supreme quality for leadership is unquestionably integrity. Without it, no real success is possible."

Dwight D. Eisenhower

A leader who is not trusted by their followers is a dictator, not a leader. In this book we have spoken about creating a vision, understanding motivation, building teams, communicating (listening and speaking), emotional intelligence, persuasion. One of the elements that has been touched on briefly in many of these is the ability and the obligation of the leader to create trust, between themselves and their followers, and between the followers.

A manager can create trust in systems and processes but a leader must create trust between people.

"Trust Rules" by Bob Lee goes into detail about all the steps a leader can take to create trust and the importance of having trust in an organisation. His studies are based on information from more than a million respondents, and one of the findings, which is unsurprising, is that people leave bosses, not companies. One of the ways to keep them, and to keep them motivated is through trust.

Some of the "rules" that he lays out in the book are:

1. Trust First: As a leader you may have to trust first before you can expect them to trust you. They are in the weaker position and generally have more to lose if they let down their guard first. Just like not trusting can be 'tit-for-tat', so can trusting. Will you be stung occasionally? Most likely, but the costs of not trusting are much higher.

2. Live with integrity: As I always say to my students, you will be working for a long time and the world is a small place. There is little to be gained from unethical short cuts. Because that leads you down a path that is both self-destructive and terrible for the world. I am not talking about being naïve, I am talking about having a personal code of ethics and values and then observing them. This is better for you personally in the long run as sometimes the most difficult person to live with is your own conscience, and from a practical point of view because followers are always more likely to trust someone they can see have a strong sense of integrity.

3. Keep your promises: A step that you have to take here is to avoid making promises in the first place. I once prided myself on following through on all my promises. At some point with the busy-ness of life I realised that I was stretching myself too thin and making too many commitments that were not possible to meet in the 24 hours of a normal day (sometimes you squeeze in 25 or 26!). I have discovered that a step towards building Trust is to say No more often, no matter how much you want to help. It is a lesson that I am still learning. I find it particularly difficult because I believe I have a responsibility to others. However a responsibility to everyone is broken promises to some – it is inevitable. And people remember those broken promises, no matter how small.

4. Involve people in decisions that affect them: This means that they can offer suggestions and ideas. It means they participate in the process. It does not mean that they take the final decision.

5. Make your expectations clear: Ken Blanchard[35] goes through in detail the different conversations you should have with a follower or employee depending on their motivation and ability. Part of this conversation is establishing what you expect from the follower – and also what you expect to give them. If you feel that they are relatively autonomous then you

---

[35] "The One Minute Manager" looks at how each employee/follower should be treated and 'led' depending on their particular situation and circumstances.

should communicate that you will be checking in only occasionally and the rest of the time you trust them to get on with things. If you do not, there is a good chance that they will feel that you have abandoned them.

You also have to be clear about you expect from them, the objectives they have to achieve, the time they have to complete them (the SMART goals are very useful here), and what 'success' looks like for you so that they know when they have achieved it. This also puts pressure on you as a leader to have a vision of what you want from them, rather than simply 'be at work' or 'be physically present'.

6. Nobody's job is 'just' anything: connected to the idea of everyone does real work, is the idea that everyone's work is important, because everyone is contributing in some way, no matter how small, to the overall vision of the collective.

7. Treat everyone fairly: This has a double meaning. Treat everyone with respect, regardless of their gender, religion or ethnic origins. No one should be given preferential treatment because this will build up resentment and internal divisions. If someone feels they should have got a pay rise or promotion or a particular job be very clear about the reasons why they did not get it, or else they may feel they are being treated unfairly.

The other meaning of treat everyone fairly is that you should not treat everyone the same. If someone leaves early they should not receive the same pay as someone who works better and longer hours. If someone does not complete their objectives then they should not automatically be given a bonus. People are treated equally but rewarded according to what they do.

8. Do what you are paid to do: People may like you, have a good time with you, think you have a great division and you have wonderful communication skills. But if you do not do what you are paid to then they will not trust you. Make sure you are clear yourself about what you are expected to do and do it. Making promises to others and keeping them is also about fulfilling your contractual obligations, without excuses.

Ethics and values

The last recession laid bare the greed and unscrupulous behaviour of many at the top. The leaders of the future were burned by that and aghast at the lack of moral compass of those at the top. While many older people complain about the 'snowflake' generation it has been correctly pointed out[36] that the Baby Boomer generation is the first generation to give absolutely nothing to the younger generation. They created a

---

[36] Thank you Julio De Castro for bringing my attention to this.

parasitical financial system, a broken housing market, a damaged atmosphere, a depleted planet.

There is an interesting book called 'I take offence at that' by Claire Fox which looks at the younger generation around the world with a very sceptical eye, at how easily upset they are by everything. In fairness to many of them, they were brought up with many things to find offense at.

What is clear however is that the leaders of today are scrutinised for their values and ethical beliefs more than ever before. No longer is 'profit maximisation' a justification for every kind of behaviour, ethical or otherwise. People want leaders who have strong morals, an acceptance of diversity, a sustainable outlook on the planet, and a moral compass that guides not only themselves, but others.

Money in the bank was an objective for a while, but the bank is broken. The Emperor does indeed have clothes, but now he has to justify where he got them from.

Key Takeaways

1. A leader must build trust with followers as opposed to just using authority.
2. This is achieved through doing things such as trusting first and living with integrity.
3. It is necessary in the 21st Century to be an ethical leader with values that your followers trust and believe in.

18

Amir

Tariighpeyma:

A man of values

Alba Blanco Iglesias

In his book, "The Little Prince", Antoine de Saint - Exupéry writes the famous phrase:

"What makes a desert beautiful is that it hides a well somewhere."

This phrase may contain dramatic connotations, but also hides a message of hope, motivation, and improvement. In my opinion, it means that, in the midst of darkness, in the midst of all those fears that hold us back, and discouragement, there is the possibility of finding some light or a gateway to self-realization.

He found it. He managed to find that well of water in the desert, and I am not talking about the little prince, but the 11-year-old boy who, in the middle of 1979, in the middle of the Iran Revolution, was able to move forward and overcome the war and the great social discontent that fueled the country, thanks to books.

At that time, our protagonist was in the middle of a crisis in the Islamic world and at a global level. Iran was at war with its eastern neighbors: Iraq, Syria and the Persian Gulf. Moreover, Iran had the leading economic power, the USA against it. On the other hand, the Islamic movement was expanding, and the monarchy of Shah Mohammed Reza Pahlavi was falling apart. Panic, fear, and rage flooded the streets. The revolutionaries who sought change wanted to establish the Islamic regime at all costs. Due to all these events, Iran was vulnerable. Civil unrest filled the streets, some of them ending in violence and death. A time of no control which our hero had to deal with. A desert from which he had to escape.

Books such as "The Autobiography of Winston Churchill" and "Capital" by Karl Marx served as multipurpose tools. They became the Swiss Army knife with which to face the world, with which to break through in that desert. They became our hero's friends, and fellow travelers, as well as a great source of information, ideas, and concepts. These books, like many others, helped to build and forge his personality, ambitions, and thoughts. With these, finally, he found the well in the desert.

Although he was still studying at school his ability to consume books and get ideas and teachings from them made him an important person to consider. Someone to listen to. He tells us in his own words, in an interview, when we asked him about his first steps towards leadership:

> *"It might sound presumptuous but those who know me, know what I am talking about. I was 11 years old, this was the Iranian revolution, and there were a lot of difficulties and trouble. At the age of 12, I had already read "Capital" by Karl Marx and other books that made a deep impacted on me ... So, at that age I used to argue with university students, and what I understood and learned that they would listen to what I have to say and make a difference. That was the first sign of so-called leadership."*

After forty years, that 12-year-old boy who took his first steps towards leadership has managed to become the leader we currently know.

Amir Tarighpeyma, born in the 60s, flew to Spain, graduated in Medicine and obtained his doctorate. In addition, he completed two Masters, one in Business Management, and the other in Hospital Management, which led him to devote the rest of his life to medicine.

Engaged in creating changes and sharing the location of the desert well, Amir began to teach economics classes to younger generations, another of his passions. Through great enthusiasm and overwhelming energy, he was able to get his students motivated and begin the search for the key that will open the doors to a life full of emotion, happiness, and success. But apart from teaching economics and promoting interest among his students, Amir also teaches them other skills, such as management, one of the main characteristics that a leader should possess.

Naturally, a leader is not only based on how capable he is at managing situations and problems. A leader requires many other facets, and he, as a good leader with years of experience, tells us which are the most important from his point of view:

"The idea of a leader or what we understand of a leader today has nothing to do with what it used to be. The leaders that I admire are not the leaders that people admire today. In other words, there are lots of leaders today, mainly entrepreneurs that there is a common admiration of these leaders. In my time, they were philosophers and politicians... there is a big difference. Things change over time. So, what makes a great leader? Good question... A great leader is the one who envisions, sets interactions, creates commitment and conviction for that to happen. This is what a great leader should do."

At the same moment, when he stops speaking, the atmosphere became rarefied. Not in a negative way. On the contrary, those last words had created an atmosphere of progression and improvement. It was as if in the middle of the room in which we were, a great mountain sprang from it, in which, if you reached the top you would become a great leader … and Amir had given us the key to achieving it. Initially, I thought that the clues that he had entrusted to us were the same characteristics that he had mentioned in his last two sentences:

> *"A great leader is the one who envisions, sets interactions, creates commitment and conviction for that to happen. This is what a great leader should do."*

But while all these elements are essential to constitute and characterize a leader, such as the fact of visualizing the context of the situation or the future of it and thus, be able to guide the rest of the team in the right direction; or even creating sufficient interactions to carry out the necessary actions, which means creating the necessary environment of commitment and conviction to achieve the objective visualized and pursued.   If all of this true but there is no capacity that allows the establishment of a firm channel of communication, that transmits and therefore shows these important qualities of true leadership, then this will be limited without a clear **path and effective application. Hence, it will simply be some kind of** theoretical or Platonic leadership.

For this reason, the ability to communicate is intrinsically linked to the rest of the qualities of a transforming and charismatic leader that can generate changes. In this sense, I wanted to understand if the man sitting in front of me considered himself a leader and if the communication skills he seemed to have were inherited or learned from one of his books.

"Well, it depends on what you define leadership to be... Entrepreneurship today creates a leadership style. In that case, yes, I consider myself a leader. According to the people I teach, the people I live with, the people I work with... yes, they would say I am a leader. A leader who envisions an idea, someone who wakes up every morning with the idea of making a change, and that is one of the reasons I love teaching."

His answer did not deviate from what I initially thought he would say. In fact, it had only been a simple question to understand if the words he used when answering were selected accurately and conscientiously. Once again, his way of speaking caught my attention, and I could not resist asking him if he had been influenced or inspired by someone when it comes to transmitting ideas or communicating with others. Amir answered the following:

"Oh yeah, definitely Winston Churchill, that is the leader I admire. We don't see those leaders anymore. Winston Churchill was a novelist, was a politician and above all, someone whose communication skills was unique. You won't see anyone like that, in my personal opinion, of course.

Winston Churchill had a lot of different moments in his life where he made a difference in the lives of others. When he realized he could not get the US involved in any war, it was Britain against Germany, he got the Canadians to get involved. And then, further on, he moved everything in his hands to make other parts of Europe join. That's leadership. He moved entire nations to do that. Part charisma, part communication, and part the fact that he was able to successfully transmit that message."

Moving away from the descriptive approach of what leadership is, I decided to address the practical part, from contemplation to implementation. In this context, it is about identifying examples or main approaches, about how our main character has defined his leadership:

"Every single time I wake up, I want to make a change. In every session of our lives, you need to make changes. Otherwise, it becomes a

one-way road with no passion, no ideas. Making a change is a difficult task. Have I made changes? The answer is yes. I have made changes and I do make changes... In the academic world to my students, in my personal role to people who surround me, my daughters... it's not easy. How to lead that change? I think one of the biggest problems we have today is leading a change in communication. Look, if we don't respect the people in front of us you can't lead change. Do I try to lead that change? The answer is yes, by achieving credibility with what I do.

If the people in front of you don't respect you, you won't lead the change no matter how well you try. Leading a change is very much linked with conviction and motivation. Do I motivate people? The answer is no. I'll tell you why, let me show you what that means. If you do something right, you would expect people to say good job, right? People today are not concerned about success, they are concerned about failure. What we worry about is not to be successful. Look, every single step in our lives is a success, every time we achieve a job, a salary, that is a success. But no, people are afraid of failing while they do that. Leading a change means making them not worry too much about the failure, but to achieve their own personal success."

In this way, Amir shows on the map the location of the water well to his closest people. He had already buried those fears of failure in the sand. Now, he wants to help others to continue the path to success. In fact, as his inspiring leader, Winston Churchill said:

"Success is not the end, failure is not fatal: it is the courage to continue that counts."

In short, the key to success is to take failures and learn from them. Fearing failure will only create more barriers on the way to your main objective, or at least, it is how I interpreted those words.

19

Doing the Hard Things

The art of leadership is saying no, not saying yes. It is very easy to say yes.

Tony Blair

Ultimately, leadership is not about glorious crowning acts. It's about keeping your team focused on a goal and motivated to do their best to achieve it, especially when the stakes are high and the consequences really matter. It is about laying the groundwork for others' success, and then standing back and letting them shine.

Chris Hadfield

If being a leader was all easy, inspirational stuff, then there would be a lot more leaders out there. The reasons there are not is because being a leader is all about being there in the valleys as well as the peaks. In the dedication at the front I said that a true a leader stood behind others when things went well but stood in front of them when they went badly. Being a leader is stepping up when others will not. It can be the hardest part of being a leader. Because when you do the hard things it is not about being a bully, or cruel, or rough with others. It is about retaining your humanity while facing the difficult situation or reality. It is about standing on the anvil, waiting for the hammer to drop, not while wearing a suit of armour but naked.

These situations include negative feedback sessions, letting someone go, disciplining them, announcing pay cuts or negative changes in working conditions, or perhaps going through a person crisis, sure that you cannot continue and then getting up and going back to the grindstone because that is your responsibility as the leader. Others have the luxury of following your lead, but you have to show them the way, even when everything else in your life is crumbling down.

Accountability

If the team or group of people are completely behind a common vision and everyone knows their role in it, then there should be no problems of accountability as everyone knows that they have to step up to make the vision a reality. I emphasis the word 'should' because that doesn't always happen. For whatever reason, it is a common problem on teams that some people do not pull their weight, make avoidable mistakes through laziness or lack of commitment, bring negative energy and a 'cannot' and 'will not' attitude to the task at hand.   It is in these moments that a leader has to roll up their sleeves and step forward.

The tools at hand can range from a frank discussion and hard feedback session (see below in difficult conversations) to formal warnings and even firing the other person.

If you let someone who is slacking continue to do so than you are rewarding destructive behaviour. Everyone else is faced with a variety of options: Continue working despite the unfairness of the situation and resent you and the other person. Start slacking themselves, knowing that there will be no punishment. Leave for another place where everyone is treated fairly.   Clearly, none of these options are good. However, for many, facing up to the individual in question can be an uncomfortable stressful situation.   But the short term pain is necessary for he continued gain of the group.   In informal groups this can be one of the most difficult conversations that you can have.

Difficult Conversations

Kerry Patterson had her fellow writers define a Crucial Conversation as one where[37]:

- There are high stakes/result is important
- They are emotionally charged

---

[37] Crucial Conversations by Patterson, Grenny, Mc Millan and Switzler is an essential additional to every leader's collection.

- Opinions differ

Something else to take into account with these exchanges is that there are three levels to the conversation[38]:

1. The 'what happened' conversation. This is about the interpretation of the facts of the situation under discussion. In the case of one involving negative feedback it is possible that the follower thinks they are doing a great job, you do not.

2. The 'feelings' conversation. This refers to the emotions that run through the conversation. Remembering back to the chapter on Emotional Intelligence, this refers to how involved our inner chimpanzee is in the conversation. If it is a high stakes conversation then the probability is high that the chimpanzee is wide awake.

3. The 'identity' conversation. How does this conversation link to the perception that the speakers have of each other and of themselves. Is this conversation precisely about differences they both have in that perception, or is one side challenging the other's identity? Using the same example as before, is it possible that the worker will react aggressively because they have a self-image of being a very hard,

---

[38] "Difficult Conversations: How to Discuss What Matters Most" by Douglas Stone, Bruce Patton, Sheila Heen is another classic that will help you deal with these situations.

conscientious person and you are threatening that by accusing them of not pulling their weight?

You should employ the listening techniques discussed in the chapter on communication to discover what the other side perceives to be 'the truth' of the situation. Remember – simply listening to their point of view does not mean that you agree with them. At this point you are simply trying to get as much information about the situation as possible. This way you will get an idea of their thought processes, and possibly where the errors are in their thinking. Equally possible is the situation where you discover facts that you were unaware of that makes you realise that *you* might be in the wrong, not them. If you have started from a position of honestly trying to get a better idea of the whole picture rather than attacking them, then if you have to accept they are right you do not have to do it by backing down or giving in.

By listening to the other first you will also create a more open atmosphere where they feel that you have understood them before you come back with your own comments. It also increases the likelihood that you can calm down their chimpanzee sufficiently so that when you start speaking to them, you are speaking to the human inside them.

At that point when you speak to them, you will have to be careful of your language. Label their feeling in a non-threatening way 'I have the impression/get the feeling that you are upset.' This is safer than 'You are upset.' They can correct your impression but they will react against your statement.

Avoid saying 'You should, you must, you have to' and simply spell out processes. 'If we want this then this is going to have to happen.'

You can also use what politicians call 'the exonerative tense' to shift the focus away from the past problems to future solutions. 'Mistakes were made', 'the product was not delivered on time', 'the work was not done' – 'now, what can we do to make sure this doesn't happen again' or 'how can we fix this in future.'

By referring to the shared purpose of the team and the organisation and using "we" you can show them that the problem they have created is affecting everyone but that they also want the solution. 'We all want a company where x happens.' 'This company is about x and I know you believe that too.' 'We are in this together and it's no-one's interest that some people ...'

William Ury also suggests a clear and easy formula for dealing with difficult situations. The Yes, No, Yes? Formula.[39] Yes) You refer to your values, the values of the organisation or the values of your team (hard work, fairness, customer satisfaction, ethical behaviour etc.) and No) you state that because of this you cannot accept X or you will have to say No etc. but that Yes?) this other possibility exists (working harder, speaking to the rest of the team about reorganising roles, leaving the company

---

[39] The Power of a Positive No by William Ury is very useful in negotiations specifically but also in any other situation where you simply feel uncomfortable saying No.

to pursue their personal goals somewhere else, would all be possible options).

Throughout all of this you will need to monitor your own emotions and reactions. You cannot react and echo their strong feelings. You cannot get defensive. It always means monitoring your body language and facial expression as they will also be hyper-sensitive to your non-verbals as well. That means adopting a positive, problem solving frame of mind so that this is reflected externally. If you fill your brain with thoughts of frustration, scorn or indifference, this will leak out in your gestures and facial tics. The focus has to remain firmly on the other person and the objective you have for this conversation, not on you.

Finally, you should be completely honest with them. This does not mean giving them all the information you have (you might have to say 'I'm not in a position to disclose that at present') but it does mean that you should not lie to them, even if you think that it's to save their feelings. You can give negative feedback, framed positively, but if they walk out of a meeting with you thinking that they are doing everything perfectly and that they do not have to change anything, or that their job is not at risk, or that they continue to slack off, then you have not done your job correctly. You have made them feel good so that they will continue to like you and not get upset with you, not because you are genuinely worried about them.

Getting up and going on.

When we speak about 'doing the hard thing' we also refer to the fact that leaders go on when others cannot, get up when others are sleep and as Simon Sinek says 'leaders eat last'.[40]

A leader has to set an example worth following. That means living the values that they are trying to convince others to adopt. If the leader expects everyone to do equal amounts of real work, then they cannot be seen to be sitting back and watching others.

Elsewhere in this book it has been said that a leader has to look after their own physical and mental health because they cannot count on others to be there for them. That is their job.

While my experience has shown me that a certain degree of vulnerability is acceptable, people tend to not feel inspired by a total basket case who is less able to cope with life's difficulties than the people they purport to lead.

If you are not prepared to shoulder the burden of leadership with all it entails then maybe you should consider stepping back from the role. However, time and again I have seen that true leaders are unable to abandon others and their responsibility for an easier life. It is that choice, to stand against

---

[40] "Leaders Eat Last" by Simon Sinek is another thought provoking book from the author of 'Start with Why'. Sinek does not write like an academic but he always makes you think.

the storm, whatever that storm may be, that truly defines a leader, more than any of the skills that I have mentioned here.

Francisco Luzón, the subject of the next chapter, personifies the indomitable spirit of a true leader, who never gives up, however hard the anvil, however heavy the hammer.

Key Takeaways

1. Being a leader is also about doing the hard things.
2. You have to hold people on the team accountable.
3. Understand the three levels of a difficult conversation.
4. Use the Yes! No! Yes? Formula when saying NO.
5. The leader is the one who stands against the storm and turns up when everyone else is still sleeping.

20

Francisco Luzón: Never Give Up

Carlota García Pleijlar
Lucía Eugena Rosado
Mario García Atucha
Pedro Figueroa Mijares

Francisco Luzón is an internationally recognised leader in the banking sector. His actions have set a difference in the history of Spanish banking. By transferring the Spanish banking system to South America, he has helped not only create a number of jobs, but inspired many to become leaders and help others. Although he is widely known in the banking sector, his name reaches further than just the entities he worked in, such as BBVA, and Santander. A few months after retiring, Francisco was diagnosed with ALS, also known as Amyotrophic Lateral Sclerosis. According to the *National Institute of Neurological Disorders and Stroke*, ALS is a "group of rare neurological diseases, which mainly involve the neurons responsible for controlling voluntary muscle movements" There is currently no cure for this disease and nothing to stop its downward progression. Thus, symptoms will progressively get worse over time. ASL is not generally considered a very well-known disease and many sufferers do not have anyone or anything to turn to for not only physical, but psychological help. However, rather than accepting this fate, Francisco recognised that the system currently in place was not able to deal with chronically ill people. This finally led him to feel obligated to take action.

After his diagnosis, Francisco realised that he could use his network from the banking world to create a foundation for sufferers from ASL, which would hopefully then be taken into consideration and called for the attention of influencers, politicians and scientists among others. Francisco created a safe environment, in which individuals, as well as their friends and family can go to share their experiences. Moreover, donations can be made towards research for the disease. The foundation has specific values, objectives, missions and visions. Objectives for the foundations include shortening waiting times and easing the process for sufferers and their families. As well as to "unite, align and encourage national research groups dedicated to ALS, whilst connecting them with the leading international lines of research". Therefore, raising awareness for the disease as well as money for finding a cure. From the information aforementioned, it is evident that Francisco is a strong minded individual, who possesses the qualities of a true leader. Not only did he create a number of jobs through changing the banking system, but he saw a clear problem and took direct action to make a change. Francisco saw a problem with the Spanish healthcare system, in that it was not equipped to deal with the effects of a chronic illness. Therefore, creating the foundation provides the support that the Spanish healthcare system cannot provide. However, one cannot simply make this change. We decided to interview Francisco and find out first-hand what he believes makes him such an effective leader.

It is important to note that Francisco was very sick and thus, was not able to write, talk, or move. This forced him to answer our questions in a unique manner: employing a system, known as *Tobii PC Eye* which enabled him to answer questions by using only his eyes. In the interview, he was asked about what steps he took to change his vision. In addition to this, we asked him what he believes are important values for a leader to possess. We found that Francisco valued teamwork, loyalty and drive in his employees extremely highly. Throughout this chapter, we will not only cover what key aspects an individual should demonstrate when working in a team, but what differentiates an individual from a leader.

The interview

The commitment was mutual: "They trusted me and my project and I trusted them."

As mentioned, in order to answer our questions, Francisco employed a technology he had not yet tried. Recently, Francisco purchased a new technology (known as *Tobii PC Eye*), which allows him to write by tracking his eye movements. We asked him questions related to leadership, working in teams, his foundation's creation and his professional life. His answers have been translated from the original interview in Spanish and summarized in the following section.

Q1. What aspects/attitudes do you consider are fundamental in order to become a leader?

Without doubt, in order to be a leader one has to be an *honest, caring* and *exemplary* person.

Q2. What helped you the most to reach the highest point in your career?

I personally accomplished that by conducting my life according to certain principles and values (respecting others, the creation of value, etc.) to which I never gave up. This were persistent throughout my life at both my job and home. Moreover, the values of effort, persistence when reaching objectives and knowing how to take advantage of opportunities, pushed me to progress until reaching the top of the Spanish and Latin American financial system.

Q3. Have you ever felt appreciated by your employees?

One of the greatest rewards that my professional life has given me is receiving gestures of gratitude and support from my employees. I received these and felt them in a very special way when I was president of Argentaria and the head of Banco Santander in Hispanoamerica. *The commitment was mutual.* They trusted me and my project and I trusted them.

Q4. As a leader, did you promote working in teams?
Without doubt, the key to success in my professional life was to ALWAYS work in teams. This has been a determinant in order to achieve the ambitious objectives that I always had and nearly always attained. My success was never mine. It always belonged to the great teams of professionals that I surrounded myself with; protagonists of my professional life. They were the ones who aided me to "swim against the current" within the financial system.

Q5. Who was fundamental in your team and why?
I always lived close to my workers because you either keep in touch with reality and touch it yourself, or you can commit enormous errors. Having said this, I always took into account the group of directives from what I used to call the "first line of direction". Effort, commitment, perseverance and the will to achieve objectives were the things that united us.

Q6. How did you select the members of your team?
I began by creating a small team at Banco Vizcaya, which then turned into the seed to form, select and promote new and young managers and directors. The most important part was that I never delegated that management function, but I always took it on myself. A big part of those people accompanied me in my change from BBVA to Banco Exterior de España, Argentaria and Santander. They believed in my projects and trusted me. Many of them worked with me for 30 years.

Q7. What would you emphasize as one of your main achievement/experiences in regards to your professional life?

It is difficult for me to choose, because there were many. But I will pick two: the creation, development and consolidation of Argentaria as the second financial institution in the Spanish banking system; and making Santander the biggest bank in Latin America. I have picked these two because of the great amount of economic and social value that generated.

Q8. How would you define/summarise your experience as a leader of the Spanish Banking System?

I would define myself as big *transformer* of the realities that I confronted. I never defined myself as a banker but as this transformer, creator of value for the business world and the society as a whole.

Q9. In regards to your foundation: did your background as an international leader smooth the process of creating the foundation? (I.e. your network, leadership skills, experience, etc.)

My long and intense professional life has taught me to look at things from a global perspective. To find the positive side of a cruel illness has made my foundation become my vital project. Today, I am a patient with ASL. Without a doubt, my international experience has helped me very much in understanding and assimilating both the illness but also the creation of the foundation; which has not only a Spanish but also a global focus.

In regards to networking, ASL was an invisible illness that has now turned into a reality in the political agenda of our country. My professional life has given me the access and capacity to make an ignored reality something well-known.

Q10. What advice would you give to future/potential leaders?
I have three pieces of advice. One, always work in teams. Two, be exemplary and faithful to your values. And three, be ambitious and persevering in your objectives but always do it for pleasure.

Fundación Luzón

The foundation's current website is: https://ffluzon.org

In it, one can learn about the objectives, mission, vision and structure of the organization. Although the opportunities this website provides go beyond that. It allows patients and their families to share their stories and experiences; the reader to sign up to a volunteering opportunity; updates and news related to the fight against ASL; and has an option to donate money to the foundation. Moreover, the foundation's ambassadors and other details regarding their initiatives and the illness itself may be found. The website succeeds in creating a space in which it is possible for a new community to be born. It has the ability to perform as a bridge between the different members of a community. A community composed by the patients of ASL and their families, the uninformed seeking for knowledge -or an opportunity to aid in making a difference-, and the ambassadors.

The project

It was an honour to be able to have a conversation with someone that has so much to say. A man who may struggle physically as a consequence of the illness he suffers but that will take the time to make sure he delivers his message in the right manner. Francisco and everyone who was involved in helping us to carry out the project were very cooperative and charming during all of it. Most importantly, as we carried out every task and moved forward towards the creation of this chapter, we learned about leadership, the importance of one's principles and values, and social skills. As a team, we are glad we have been able to contribute in our own way to this community and hope for the Fundación Luzón to continue its fight against ASL by continuing to raise awareness, maintain its focus and reach its objectives.

Sources

"Amyotrophic Lateral Sclerosis (ALS) Fact Sheet." National Institute of Neurological Disorders and Stroke, U.S. Department of Health and Human Services, www.ninds.nih.gov/Disorders/Patient-Caregiver-Education/Fact-Sheets/Amyotrophic-Lateral-Sclerosis-ALS-Fact-Sheet.

"The Luzón Foundation Joins the Science Foundations Council." Fundación Luzón, ffluzon.org/en/the-luzon-foundation-joins-the-science-foundations-council/.

Conclusion:

So what next?

Leadership is a choice, not a position.

Stephen Covey

This book is about real leaders, real people and real skills. It does not pretend to be an academic tome, or a ground breaking piece of research. Its goals are more modest, but hopefully the stories here and the takeaways at the end of each skills chapter, mean that there is a greater chance you will see yourself as a leader and take on the role with a more conscious sense of purpose from now on.

When I began to think of leaders as something more than the president of a company or a multinational or some historic figure that led troops into battle, when I realised that being a leader was not the same as being a manager, it was then that I began to see leaders all around me:

The career diplomat who listened to me, acknowledged what I said without having to agree, built trust with me through empathy and a shared vision and then inspired me to achieve my goals. She is the perfect example of a Servant leader.

Amparo Vera, the vice-director of ICEX-CECO, buried deep in the forest, ensuring incremental change in a complex web of upward and downward links, leading everyone towards a vision of a brighter, selfless future.

Luisa Barón, head of faculty at IE, organising over a thousand people with diplomacy and care, treating everyone as an individual and taking into account their personalities, their motivations and their foibles. With an ability to maintain an overall goal for her organisation while remembering the smallest detail about everyone she is over. Putting herself second and her 'faculty family' first. A daily inspiration.

Jessica Linville, managing diversity, setting goals, never leaving until the job is done, injecting her troops with energy and passion for their work. She always stands between them and the bullets that come from every direction. She leads through example on a daily basis.

Daria Dixon, a Level 5 leader in training. Standing in a refugee camp on Christmas day, holding a malnourished baby in her arms. Bringing strength and hope to others and leading because she stands up when others would sit back. I cannot wait to see how she will change the world for the better.

Cristina Manso, leading her family and her own company. First up in the morning, last to bed at night. Sacrifice, doing the hard thing and leading through serving. A reminder that a mother who gives up her job should never put a gap on their C.V. as they learn emotional intelligence, conflict resolution, team building, listening skills, and motivation – all done on battle naps.

When I read the stories in this book and see leaders through the eyes of those who will themselves lead and have already taken their first steps in leadership I realise that they have found the truth - leaders are not the people we see on television, they are the people we meet every day, and we have so much to learn from them.

When you develop your emotional intelligence, when you help persuade a friend to take a better course of action, when you bring your indoor football club together as a team to celebrate a victory (or overcome a loss), when you tell a loved one that their actions have hurt you and they will have to change, when you decide to stop eating chocolates for a month and you create a plan to get through it, when you volunteer for a charity without anything in return. When you do all of these things and a million others, you are practising leadership skills and you are preparing for the day when you are the one appearing in a story in a book like this.

There is a leader inside of you, and it is my sincere hope that after reading this book and the stories in it, that you recognise that side of yourself, embrace it and will it to grow.

Brendan Anglin

May 2018

"A leader is one who knows the way, goes the way, and shows the way."

John C. Maxwell

"Leadership and learning are indispensable to each other."

John F. Kennedy

...and one final word of thanks to Lucas, a leader whose story is still being written. You are holding this book in your hands because of all his efforts. When people ask me for an example of a leader, I look around, see him and point.

Select Bibliography

Adair, J. (2005)*How to Grow Leaders*   Kogan Page

Alder, H. & Heather, B. (1999) *NPL in 21 days* Piatkus

Belbin, M. (2004) *Management Teams* Elservier Butterwort-Heinemann

Berne, E. (1964) *Games people play* Penguin Books

Borg, J. (2007) *Persuasion* Pearson

Briffa, J. (2014) *A great day at the office* Fourth Estate

Campbell, A. (2016) *Winners and how they succeed* Arrow books

Carnegie, D. (1936) *How to win friends & influence people* Pocket Books

Carson, M. (2013) *The Managers* Bloomsbury

Covey, S. (2004) *The 7 Habits of highly effective people* Simon & Schuster

Coyle, D. (2013) *The Green Platform* Ballpoint Press

Dalio, R. (2017) *PRINCIPLES* Simon & Schuster

De Bono, E. (2004) *How to have a beautiful mind* Vermilion

Duhigg, C. (2012) *The Power of Habit. Why we do what we do and how to change*   Random House

Dutton, K. (2010) *Flipnosis* Arrow books

Fisher, R . and Ury, W. and Patton, B. (1991) *Getting to Yes* Penguin Books

Fisher, R. & Shapiro, D. (2007) *Building agreement* Random House

Gaffney, M. (2012) *Flourishing* Penguin Books

Goleman, D. (1995) *Emotional Intelligence* Bantam Books

Goulston, M. (2010) *Just Listen* Amacom

Heath, C. & Heath, D. (2007) *Made to Stick* Random House

Jeffers, S. (1991) *Feel the fear and do it anyway* Arrow books

Johnson, S. (1999) *Who Moved my Cheese* Vermilion

Kahneman, D. (2011) *Thinking, Fast and Slow* Penguin Books

Kouzes, J. & Posner, B. (2017) *The leadership challenge* Leadership Challenge

Krogerus, M. & Tschäppeler (2011) *The Decision Book* Profile Books

Krznaric, R. (2014) *Empathy, A handbook for Revolution* Random House

Lee, B. (2017) *Trust rules* Trust Lab Press

Lehrer, J. (2010) *How we decide* Mariner Books

McCann´s, D. (2003) *Business Bathroom Bible* The   Liffey press

Mcgrath, J. & Bates, B. (2017) *The little book of big management theories* Pearson

Michalko, M. (2006) *Thinkertoys* Ten speed press

Miller, P. (2008) *The really good fun Cartoon Book of NLP* Crown House

Northouse, P. (2016) *Leadership Theory and Practice* SAGE

O´connor, J.& Lages, A. (2004) *Coaching With NPL* Harper Element

O´Connor, J.& Seymour, J. (1990) *Introducing NLP* Harper Element

Patterson, K.; Grenny, J.; McMillan, R.; Switzler, A. (2012) *Crucial Conversations* Mc Graw Hill

Peters, S. (2013) *The chimp paradox* Tarcher Penguin

Pink, D. (2010) *Drive* Canongate

Robbins, A. (1997) *Unlimited Power* Fireside Simon & Schuster

Scouller, J. (2011) *The Three Levels of Leadership* Management books 2000

Shell, R. & Moussa, M. (2007) *The art of woo* Penguin Books

Sinek, S. (2009) *Start with why* Porfolio Penguin

Sinek, S. (2017) *Leaders eat last* Porfolio Penguin

Starr, J. (2016) *The coaching manual*   Pearson

Stone, D. & Heen, S. (2014) *Thanks for the feedback* Porfolio Penguin

Taylor, D. (2007)   *The naked coach: business coaching made simple* Capstone

Ulrich, D. ;Smallwood, N. and Sweetman, K.   (2008)   *The Leadership Code, Five rules to lead by*   Harvard   Business Review Press

Whitmore, J. (2017)   *Coaching for Performance*   Nicholas Brealey

Wilson, L, (2011) *The Social Styles Hand Book* Nova Vista

Zaffron, S. & Logan, Dave (2009)   *The three laws of performance* Jossey Bass

Leadership Skills and Stories